CHRISTIAN MATURITY

Bernard Häring, C.Ss.R.

CHRISTIAN MATURITY

Holiness in Today's World

St Paul Publications

St Paul Publications
Middlegreen, Slough SL3 6BT, England

Copyright © Bernard Häring 1983
First published in Great Britain February 1983
Printed by the Society of St Paul, Slough
ISBN 085439 223 8

St Paul Publications is an activity of the priests and brothers of the Society of St Paul who promote the Christian message through the mass media.

Contents

Acknowledgement

My heartfelt thanks go to Mrs Josephine Ryan who, with her usual care, polished up my English and did the final typing, and to the Lord who allowed her to do it so well in her 85th year of life.

Bernard Häring C.Ss.R.

Introduction

A short time ago the president of the University of Munich, Prof. Nikolaus Lobkowicz, was asked what kind of changes would be most needed in today's world to facilitate access to faith and peace. His response was prompt: "Radiant saints! . . . They recognize the 'signs of the times'. Without saints nothing really new and authentic will happen. True, saints are people whom God has seized and graced; but usually saints arise only where the awareness prevails that striving for holiness is an integral element of being a Christian."

This book is written to strengthen that consciousness. A previous book of mine, *Called to Holiness*, concludes with a chapter entitled, 'Holiness is Mission'. Other religions may imagine saints who simply withdraw from the world to pursue nothing more than their own salvation or quietude. Christians know that being 'chosen', being called to holiness, called, indeed, to follow Christ, is an offer open to all humankind. Holiness, in a distinctively christian sense, cannot be privatized. Hence, my aim here is to set forth in tangible form the essential social dimension of being a Christian: "to bear fruit in love for the life of the world" (Vatican II, *The Training of Priests*, 16).

There is also special need to sharpen the sensitivity of all Christians to this dimension, in view of some absurd theological assertions that give prime importance or almost exclusive attention to the need for revolutionary changes of structures. Some persons would even advocate violence as a prime instrument for saving the world, despite all the evidence that violence begets more violence and hatred and, in today's world, can lead to the self-destruction of the human race.

CHAPTER ONE

Together on the road to truth

> "Jesus replied, 'My kingdom does not belong to this world. If it did, my followers would be fighting to save me from arrest by the Jews. My kingly authority comes from elsewhere.' 'You are a king, then?' said Pilate. Jesus answered, ' "King" is your word. My task is to bear witness to the truth. For this I was born; for this I came into the world, and all who are not deaf to truth listen to my voice.' Pilate said, 'What is truth?', and with these words went out again to the Jews. 'For my part,' he said, 'I find no case against him' " (Jn 18:36-38).

THE world needs people who seek truth, the ultimate meaning of life, salvation truth, and who seek it wholeheartedly together with their fellow travellers in an authentic reciprocity of consciences.

Mature Christians know that Christ is *the Truth*. For them the one thing that matters is to know Christ and, through him, the Father, and to know ever better the origin, destiny and vocation of man.

Holy people know that they are not private owners of salvation truth. Seized by Christ and blessed by the unsurpassable knowledge of Christ, they realize that the world needs nothing more urgently than this truth, this knowledge. Their own striving for a more profound, more encompassing and vital knowledge of truth goes hand in hand, therefore, with their desire to learn with others and to help others on the road to truth.

Today's world is in a situation similar to that of Pilate's and the ruling class of Israel: their interest in truth and their allegiance to it are terribly diverted.

Faced with the greatest decision in human history, Israel's ruling class and the representative of Roman world power are thoroughly immersed in the quest for earthly power. They see truth and justice only in the perspective of their own main interests. They are unwilling and, in a certain sense, already unable to deal directly with truth and justice. A truth that does not serve their interests leaves them sceptical. Even talk on religion is, for them, an instrument of power. Thus their access to saving truth is blocked, as is also the road to justice.

Before them stands the powerless witness of the saving truth, the Truth in person. Yet through this powerlessness shines the divine majesty of salvation truth, incarnate in Jesus Christ who will seal it with his blood as Redeemer.

The 'I-am-the-Truth' of John's gospel shows us that the vital decision of every person and of humanity as a whole is made in confrontation with the truth for which they stand, live and die. "All who are not deaf to truth listen to my voice" (Jn 18:37).

Confronting the 'I-am-the-Truth' and his authentic witnesses, there is no legitimate escape into mere theoretical questions. Each of us has to make our decision about our own truth of existence, and all of us will make visible our own truthfulness or, on the contrary, our estrangement from truth. Jesus tells the Jews in scathing language why his words "make no headway with you" (Jn 8:37). They have made themselves slaves of the 'father of lies' in whom there is no truth; therefore, they are carrying out their own 'father's desires' (Jn 8:44). But those who are sincerely seeking the saving truth and acting accordingly find their home in the words of Jesus; they rejoice in hearing his voice.

The fundamental option to seek ultimate truth and meaning, and to act on them, opens the gate to the blissful reign of truth and the liberating experience of ever new horizons of truth and of knowledge of the 'I-am-the-Truth'.

With all the ardour of his love and in full awareness of his being sent by the Father, Jesus speaks about this mystery of God and man. "This is eternal life: to know thee who alone art truly God, and Jesus Christ whom thou hast sent" (Jn 17:3).

Exultingly he foretells the bliss of those who have entered into this realm of knowledge and truth. "I have taught them all that I learned from thee, and they have received it; they know with certainty that I came from thee; they have had faith to believe that thou didst send me" (Jn 17:8). And at the same time he prays fervently for his disciples, that they may trust-worthily proclaim this truth to the world which so badly needs it. "Consecrate them by the truth . . . may they all be one: as thou, Father, art in me, and I in thee, so also may they be in us, that the world may believe that thou didst send me" (Jn 17: 17–21).

One enters into this saving truth not as a result of mere human effort; it is the work of the Spirit of Truth. By one's fundamental option, made with heart, mind and will, the disciples of Christ open themselves to the promptings of the Holy Spirit. "I will ask the Father and he will give you another to be your Advocate, who will be with you for ever — the Spirit of truth. The world cannot receive him because the world neither sees nor knows him; but you know him because he dwells with you and is in you" (Jn 14: 16–17).

The 'world' of which Jesus speaks is of people locking themselves into their own pride, trusting in their own achievement. Here we easily recognize today's world of people who have become unable to transcend the realm of experimental knowledge, of truth for utility.

This world is to be changed, to be offered a new chance by the disciples of Christ. Seized by the Spirit of Truth, they will be gradually led into the full truth. "Your Advocate, the Holy Spirit whom the Father will send in my name, will teach you everything, and will call to mind all that I have told you" (Jn 14: 26). The 'everything' does not mean an encyclopedic knowledge but rather an encompassing vision of reality in the light of Christ's gospel. And that is what the world of today so urgently needs.

Through Christ's faithful disciples who entrust themselves to the power of the Spirit of Truth, this very Spirit "will confute the world, and show where wrong and right and judgement lie" (Jn 16: 8). Even those whose minds are set on self-sufficiency and self-fulfilment will be able finally to see their error, their estrangement, when faced with Christ's true disciples whose minds are set first on seeking God's kingdom and, therefore, are filled with joy, peace and love. In a world where everyone and each group seeks only their own interest, power and 'right', they come to realize how far they are from righteousness and truth. Their restless and ruthless search for more power, more possessions, more consumption, is seen in its own truth as bringing misery to themselves and others while estranging them from the saving and all-encompassing truth and justice (cf. Jn 16: 8–13).

All men of good will can learn from people who are guided by the Spirit of God — 'the Father of the poor', — that they cannot dwell in the truth unless they effectively take sides with the unloved, the oppressed, the downtrodden.

Those who are on the road of truth will understand better and better that, for their own salvation as well as for the sake of humanity, they still have to go a long way before they are completely transformed in their whole being and in all their relationships by the truth. But grace appeals to them and comes to them. "His divine power has bestowed on us everything that makes for life and true religion, enabling us to know the One who called us by his own splendour and might. Through this might and splendour he has given us his promises, great beyond all price, and through them you may escape the corruption with which lust has infected the world, and come to share in the very being of God. With all this in view, you should try your hardest to supplement your faith with virtue, virtue with knowledge, knowledge with self-control, self-control with fortitude, fortitude with piety, piety with brotherly kindness, and brotherly kindness with love " (2 Pet 1 : 3–7).

Our concern, then, must be that our 'knowledge of our Lord Jesus Christ' will not be 'useless or barren' for the life of the world (cf. 2 Pet 1 : 8), but rather fruitful in truth and love. God is love, and we are to be his image. Salvation knowledge leads us on the road of love, and as we progress in saving love, we are led to a deeper and more blissful knowledge of truth.

The apostle of the Gentiles rejoices that he is granted to impart 'wisdom', not that of the rulers of the times but "God's hidden wisdom, his secret purpose framed from the very beginning to bring us to our full glory" (1 Cor 2 : 4–7).

While today's situation is in many ways different from that of Paul's time, it is a striking and alarming sign of our times that the so-called 'developed' world makes its greatest progress in knowledge geared to material achievement and to dominion, especially right-by-might dominion. The whole educational system of the western world is for economic, professional and social success. However, the achievers and consumers which this system turns out are not on the wave-length of the wisdom that comes from God and leads to God.

Granted, structural changes of our system are surely necessary, but they will not succeed without men and women outstanding in wisdom. Christians have to become more aware of what they can and must give to the world if they are to be faithful to their calling. "This is the Spirit that we have received from God, and not the spirit of the world, so that we may know all that God, of his own grace, has given us; and because we are interpreting spiritual truths to those who have the Spirit, we speak of these gifts of God in words found for us not by our human wisdom but by the Spirit" (1 Cor 2: 12–13).

The wisdom which concerns us is not speculation about theories estranged from life, but wisdom about the destiny and calling of men and women, understood in the light of the love of the Creator and Redeemer. The Second Vatican Council speaks about this in view of our vocation to holiness. "Christ, who died and was raised up for all, can through his Spirit offer man the light and the strength to measure up to his supreme destiny. Nor has any other name under heaven been given to man by which it is fitting for him to be saved." The church "likewise holds that in her most benign Lord and Master can be found the key, the focal point, and the goal of all human history" (*The Church in the Modern World*, 10).

Nobody should dream that saints, whom humankind needs so much today, would encapsule themselves in an exclusively supernatural sphere. There is for them an effective scale of values, a wholeness of vision in which all the different kinds of knowledge have their own weight and place.

As Christians, we are open-minded to every kind of truth. We learn from humanity's historical experience made accessible to us through scientific research. We cannot disdain natural sciences that decipher many secrets, processes, reciprocities and dynamics of the created world. They not only help us to admire God's wonderful work more and more, they are also indispensable for human health, food production, and many other human needs. Nor can we neglect the behavioural sciences which improve our understanding of human development, psychic growth and social relationships.

When Christian men and women make their contribution in such fields as culture, science, economics, politics, education, the healing professions, they have to do their very best to acquire the necessary competence. Piety and good will alone are not enough.

The authentic Christian will be distinguished from the unbeliever and superficial neighbour by his or her priorities and vision of wholeness. Salvation truth comes first: to know God and to know people in the light of Christ. And Christians should never forget that salvation knowledge cannot be acquired in the same ways as knowledge for success and dominion. Since God is love, and since our vocation is to be and to become more and more an image of God, our beginning and our progress on the road of salvation truth depend on the firmness and depth of our fundamental option for redeemed and redeeming love.

This insight was sharply brought home to me by an experience in a leprosarium in India. It was there that I met a young and gifted artist from Paris. She had been brought up in total atheism. When she started to search into and to discuss religious questions, a young man told her one day with astonishing conviction: "The God in whom we believe cannot be found by mere reasoning and discussion. Since he is Love, he can be found only by loving people." She told us that this word hit her in her deepest being, and her mind worked constantly on the question, "But how can I be sure that what I intend to do is really done for love's sake?" She decided then, on the spur of the moment, to serve for one year in the rehabilitation of lepers in India, especially because of her terrible distaste for this kind of misery. At the end of the year she decided to remain there in gratitude to God and to these poor people, since they had helped her to find God — to find love.

Our devotion to truth implies a wonderful wholeness which we can describe as: to *be* truthful, to *think* truthfully, to *do* the truth and to *speak* truth.

To be truthful: The world, deceived by so many ideologies, power-structures, collective and individual egotisms, is even more in need of our 'being in the truth' than of our actions.

We can work and conduct a dialogue as Christians only if we have found and live our identity, our 'Yes' to the saving truth in Jesus Christ. To be 'in the truth' implies an absolutely sincere conscience, truthfulness to ourselves, our neighbours and to God, in a liberating reciprocity of consciences which searches for truth and acts on it in togetherness. Further, it implies fidelity, reliability, total commitment to 'do truth in love'. Truth-fulness and the transparence of our conscience coincide with the 'purity of heart', the purity of intentions and motives, so highly praised in the sermon on the mount.

As pilgrims we cannot be 'in the truth' without humbly acknowledging that we are, at best, only on the road to greater fullness of truthfulness in being and in acting. This gives us the courage to confess our sins and shortcomings, and to accept the need for further conversion to the One who can say, 'I-am-the-Truth', while praising God constantly for having called us into his wonderful light.

To think truthfully: The thinking of estranged people — superficial, distracted, even chaotic — can be greatly helped by contact with people whose minds and hearts are filled with the gladdening truth revealed in Jesus Christ. They give priority to salvation truth, and cultivate other forms of knowledge according to their scale of values and of service to love and justice. More than knowledge of what promotes their own material progress and success, they care to know God, to know Christ, to know human dignity and destiny and how to love truthfully. And out of gratitude for the knowledge received from God and through other people, they strive for ever deeper and more integrated knowledge.

A person who wants to think truthfully will also develop the contemplative dimension of human life, allowing room for silence, practising temperance in the search for news and information, and discerning what is truly worth occupying space in one's cerebral cortex and memory.

To speak truth and to do truth go hand in hand. One's face radiates purity of heart and mind or, on the contrary, the frustra-tion, restlessness, hostility of one's thoughts and intentions. Our actions are highly-qualified communications. If they arise from our being in the truth and thinking the truth in love, they generate healthy relationships and build up community in truth.

In our christian understanding, we speak truth only insofar as we speak with authentic love and in the service of love and justice. Our truthful words and actions resemble the Word incarnate who, from all eternity, is that WORD which breathes love and sends us the Spirit of Truth, enabling us to do truth in love.

Whoever uses knowledge to hurt or damage others is not in the truth, does not think truthfully, does not speak truth. Abuse of knowledge belongs to the work of the 'confuser' (*diabolos*, devil). Only truth spoken and done in love comes from God and leads to God, the Father of light.

The ministry of truth requires discretion, prudence, discernment. The disciple of Christ does not 'throw pearls to the pigs, for 'they will only trample on them' (cf. Mt 7:6). If we have to deal with people who intend to interrogate us in order to harm us or others, then this situation partially determines the meaning and manner of our discourse. Faced with those who would do evil, an answer that conceals what has to be concealed does not contradict the basic rule imparted to us by Christ: "Plain 'Yes' or 'No' is all you need to say" (Mt 5:37).

Our refusal to participate in the malice of others is a firm 'Yes' to our mission to be 'salt of the earth', a firm 'No' to the reign of darkness and the work of the 'Confuser'. This can be exemplified by the response, given by christian nurses during the reign of Hitler, to the hangmen who came to their orphanage enquiring about the number of children under their care who were affected by hereditable diseases. What they were really asking was not about sick children in need of help but simply about objects for the gas chambers and soap factories. The sisters' response to that real question could only be, "We have no such children." Holiness has nothing to do with naïvety.

*   *   *

Lord Jesus Christ, before your sacrificial death you prayed for us to the Father: 'Sanctify them in the truth!'

Send forth the Holy Spirit to lead us into a growing knowledge of your love and truth, a loving knowledge of the Father and a saving knowledge of ourselves and our brothers and sisters. Cleanse our hearts, our minds, our will through the Spirit of Truth. Help us to strive towards an ever fuller knowledge of faith and all that it implies. Bring us together on the road with you, so that we can assist each other in our love for truth and our joy in the saving truth.

Help us to rid ourselves from senseless curiosity about thousands of petty things and novelties which contribute nothing to our growth or our mission and ministry. Assist and illumine us in our striving for whatever knowledge is necessary for competent service to our fellow travellers.

Let those who know a multitude of things, but not what serves justice, love, health and salvation, realize that they are blind and truly ignorant. Grant them hunger and thirst for the essential truths.

With you, Lord Jesus, we praise the Father for having revealed the secrets of salvation to the simple ones while they remain hidden from the arrogant who boast about their wisdom (cf. Lk 10:21). Through the power of the Spirit of Truth, help us to become humble and single-minded, and make us ready to learn from the humble and the poor.

B

CHAPTER TWO

The art of dialogue

"Never remain silent when a word might put things right,
for wisdom shows itself by speech,
and a man's education must find expression in words.
Do not argue against the truth.
Never be ashamed to admit your mistakes. . . .
Be quick to listen,
but take time over your answer.
Answer another if you know what to say,
but if not, hold your tongue.
Honour and shame can come through speaking,
and a man's tongue may be his downfall.
Do not get a name for being a gossip
or lay traps with your tongue. . . .
Do not answer without first listening,
and do not interrupt when another is speaking. . . .
One man is silent and is found to be wise;
another is hated for his endless chatter.
One man is silent, at a loss for an answer;
another is silent, biding his time.
The wise man is silent until the right moment,
but a swaggering fool is always speaking out of turn.
A garrulous man makes himself detested,
and one who abuses his position arouses hatred."
(Ecclus 4 : 23–26; 5 : 11–14; 11 : 8; 20 : 5–8).

THE wise Jesus Sirach (Ecclesiasticus) shares with us these lucid observations and rules for dialogue. The art of dialogue plays an important role in assuring harmony on the road of truth. He emphasizes especially the choice of partners, the readiness to listen and to learn, and the intention to help each other in the search for wisdom.

There is an indissoluble reciprocity between our dialogue with God and our dialogue with our fellow travellers. In communion with God it is evident that the first condition is to listen and to acknowledge God's initiative. He speaks to us through all his creation, through the events of our life, our times and, last but not least, through people who have opened themselves to his wisdom and kindness. Happy are those who live with others who know how to listen to God and to make all their life a response to him!

Jesus Christ is not only the final and supreme Word spoken to us by the Father; he is also the unsurpassable master of dialogue. The incarnate Son lives wholly by the word that comes from the Father. He is the perfect listener.

To Israel, chosen to be his servant and messenger, God says: "Hear now, you that are deaf; you blind men, look and see: yet who is blind but my servant, who so deaf as the messenger whom I send?" (Is 42:18–19). But of the new Israel, the Servant, it is foretold: "The Lord God has given me the tongue of a teacher and skill to console the weary with a word in the morning; he sharpened my hearing that I might listen like one who is taught. The Lord God opened my ears and I did not disobey" (Is 50: 4–5).

The gospel shows us clearly how wonderfully Jesus has listened to the words of God in the holy scriptures, but equally how attentively he listens to wise people, to the needs of people, and to the cry of the downtrodden and sinners.

Jesus, the teacher, speaks in dialogue with his disciples and even with his opponents. He brings home the knowledge of people as fruit of his listening. He asks questions and answers questions. His dialogue meets people in their own experience and problems, and from there he leads them patiently to a deeper vision. What a wonderful example is his dialogue with the woman of Samaria! (cf. John, 4).

Dialogue is a basic human experience. It becomes the supreme human art wherever people not only speak words with each other but express themselves in openness and trust, manifesting their love and assuring each other of their fidelity.

The quality, stability and happiness of a marriage depend greatly on the quality of the dialogue between husband and wife. In a good marriage and family life, behind all the words and gestures, stands the basic communication: "It is good that you are! It is good that I can be for you!" Authentic conjugal love in all its dimensions, but especially in the conjugal embrace, is that wonderful dialogue in which the spouses open their hearts to each other and entrust themselves to each other.

Good partners, gifted with the art of dialogue, do not pull words to pieces, as untender hands sometimes do to flowers, nor do they just listen to words. They meet their partners as unique persons, with an intuitive sense of the kindness, happiness, sympathy, trouble or pain which underlies the other's words and gestures.

In its full sense, dialogue is sharing joy and sorrow with each other; it is grateful reception and enrichment not only of knowledge and experience, but also of learning to love better, with greater sympathy and reverence, and thus also to discover one's own and the other's inner being and resources.

The fruit of dialogue depends on both its content and the way it is conducted. A marriage or friendship gains much if, in the partners' dialogue, there is a sharing of high ideals, vital interests, commitment to an important cause, and a continuing search for deeper knowledge of truth and wisdom.

Dialogue between married couples and between educators can bear rich fruit in education. Happy are the children whose parents and educators are masters in dialogue, willing and able to listen to the children in their uniqueness, joys and needs, and to speak with them in such a way that they can better discover their capabilities and meet their difficulties!

Children can help us to progress in the art of dialogue and to understand what Jesus meant when he invited us to become like children, single-minded, cordial, open. The child experiences great encouragement when his or her first efforts to talk are taken seriously and are a source of joy for the family. But long before children articulate words and sentences, they are already communicating effectively in many ways their joy, fear, pain, attachment, hunger and need for love in a beginning dialogue.

If parents and educators are competent partners in dialogue, children will express themselves confidently in conversation and questions. When parents acknowledge that they do not know the right answer to a question and need time to think about it, the child begins to learn an important aspect of good dialogue. And it is even more fruitful for the child's education, as well as for all participants in the dialogue, if a parent confesses, with truthful simplicity, "I was wrong; I should not have said (or done) that; I am sorry."

Not the least of a dialogue's riches are sharing joy and opening to each other the various gateways to joy. For this a sense of humour can be a marvellous charism. Serious or difficult dialogue needs laugh-provoking punctuations by jokes, funny stories, wit; and even a dialogue of sadness needs light moments of cheer, hope, happy or humorous reminiscences or prophecies. All these can be offered by the Christian without any descent from the mount of the beatitudes.

Jesus Sirach calls our attention to the art of listening, of silence, vigilance for the right moment and the right word. To learn all this takes time and practice. We have to examine the quality of our dialogue again and again in order to improve it. Among friends, and especially between married couples, it might be advisable or even necessary sometimes to have a heart-to-heart talk about the meaning, purpose and quality of their day-by-day dialogue.

Dialogue is an expression of our complementarity. In a mature dialogue we acknowledge the other as other, and are grateful that he or she is different from us. This is particularly important in the dialogue between man and woman. It can be enriching only if both affirm, by word and deed, their equal dignity and rejoice in their diversity.

Dialogue is the proper way to prepare decisions which concern all the partners. One of the greatest evils in today's world is the arrogance of individuals and groups who decide alone about economic, cultural and political matters which deeply affect the lives of others. The decisions would be fairer and more prudent if all concerned were allowed to contribute their experiences, their competence, viewpoints and interests. It would then also be much easier to put decisions into practice.

Patient and respectful dialogue in the search for truth and for meaningful solutions to common problems is at the heart of the partnership family. The dignity of all members is thus constantly reaffirmed, and the children can gradually grow into full responsibility. Ultimately it depends upon the quality of dialogue on the family level whether the high ideals of democracy in the social, cultural and political realms can be worked out to serve genuine human development and peace.

21

A most noble form of dialogue is in sharing or communicating faith by witness and word in marriage, in the family, among friends, in prayer-groups and in direct pastoral activities. At the heart of this dialogue is a common effort to discern the events and experiences in the light of faith. Thereby we share the joy of faith and the consolation that comes from God and leads to him.

The dialogue of faith reaches particular fullness if the partners are aware that they are gathered in the name of the Lord, and he is present with them. The ideal friendship is anchored in this friendship with the Lord. The dialogue between believer-friends arises from and leads to intimate dialogue with the Lord.

Paul's first letter to the Corinthians, especially chapter 14, shows us how spontaneous and dynamic the dialogue of faith was in that early community. This called for efforts to keep it on a high level and to guarantee a minimum of order. The saint's letters indicate also that in the dialogue of faith a great diversity of charisms and experiences were included. The trust that this diversity enriched dialogue and unity was grounded in the truth that the *one* Spirit builds up unity through the very diversity of gifts and ministries, since each charism is given by the Spirit for the benefit of all.

The letter to the Philippians — in which Paul, a prisoner for the Lord's sake, gives consolation and exhortation — lays down the basic rules for the dialogue. "If then our common life in Christ yields anything to stir the heart, any loving consolation, any sharing of the Spirit, any warmth of affection or compassion, fill up my cup of happiness by thinking and feeling alike, with the same love for one another, the same turn of mind, and a common care for unity. There must be no room for rivalry and personal vanity among you, but you must humbly reckon others better than yourselves. Look to each other's interest and not merely to your own" (2:1–4).

This same vision belongs also to the fundamental law of the church universal. Those in authority depend greatly on the manifold charisms and particular competences available among the people of God. All this needs encouragement and the kind of channeling which favours creativity and makes it fruitful for the benefit of all.

The basic principles of collegiality and subsidiarity point in this direction. In the worldwide catholic church, there must be ample room even on the institutional level for dialogue among the various cultures, historical experiences, traditions, customs, competences and needs. A fanaticism for uniformity is not only an impoverishment and an enemy of love and mutual appreciation, it is anti-dialogical and, above all, a sin against the Spirit.

If the church, in her inner life, is a model of fostering and articulating dialogue on all levels, then she can also make a most valuable contribution to the promotion of dialogue within the secular world, between social classes, ethnic groups, cultures and subcultures, political parties, and even among various ideologies and worldviews. Nobody can doubt that the art of dialogue is a basic presupposition in all endeavours for peace and justice. For all these reasons the world does, indeed, need saints — masters of dialogue.

*   *   *

Lord, how wonderful it is to know that all of creation in your world and all the events of redemption are your initiative in a dialogue with us. You made us able to listen, and you assure us that you are interested in our response. In all our needs, as well as in our joys, we are encouraged to speak to you with gratitude and confidence.

Lord, teach us how to be silent before you in order to understand better your message. Speak to our hearts as well as to our minds. Move our will so that we can entrust ourselves to you and always search earnestly to understand your design for us.

We thank you, loving Father, for the gift of speech and language, for ears and tongue. Thank you for all the loving people who share with us not only their knowledge but also the art of loving, the art of listening to console and to encourage.

Lord, send forth your Spirit to teach us that art of dialogue which makes us an image and likeness of your triune life and of your loving presence among us. Teach us the kind of prayer that nourishes fruitful human dialogue, responds to your initiative, and forespeaks the eternal dialogue in the communion of saints, the eternal praise of your bounty to which you invite us even now as adorers of your divine life in word and love.

CHAPTER THREE

Rejoicing in everything that is beautiful

"So in the Spirit he carried me away to a great high mountain, and showed me the holy city of Jerusalem coming down out of heaven from God. It shone with the glory of God; it had the radiance of some priceless jewel, like a jasper, clear as crystal. . . . The wall was built of jasper, while the city itself was of pure gold, bright as clear glass. The foundations of the city wall were adorned with jewels of every kind, the first of the foundation-stones being jasper, the second lapis lazuli, the third chalcedony, the fourth emerald, the fifth sardonyx, the sixth cornelian, the seventh chrysolite, the eighth beryl, the ninth topaz, the tenth chrysoprase, the eleventh turquoise, and the twelfth amethyst. The twelve gates were twelve pearls, each gate being made from a single pearl. The streets of the city were of pure gold, like translucent glass" (Rev 21: 10-11; 18-21).

HOLINESS shows no sour face. If the all-holy God draws us totally to himself in order to make us a shining light for the world, then he does so by the splendour of his bounty, his bliss and the attractive power of all the beauty he has revealed. To rejoice in beauty is an essential dimension of humanness. If this is missing or inert, there is no pathway to the morality of the beatitudes and the praise of God's glory.

Someone had brought a beautiful bouquet of flowers to the sickbed of a patient who was a heavy smoker and drinker. He did not even look at them, but curtly told the nurse to take them away, saying: "What good are these flowers? I can't eat, drink or smoke them!"

Of course, nothing is to be said against the good taste of wine and food which are also God's gifts, a foreshadowing of the heavenly feast and a reminder of the eucharistic meal; but how could one imagine the joyous banquet with God and all his saints if one's pleasure is restricted to what one can eat, smoke or drink? How wretched is the person who cannot rejoice in beauty, bounty, signs of friendship, who cannot admire and be grateful for what is good, true and beautiful in itself! Nothing is left to him but the hangover and boredom.

Our sick man, who sees no meaning in beautiful flowers, is by chance not only a heavy consumer but, in healthy days, he was also an achiever, a hard worker, boasting of his sense of duty. He is representative of a substantial part of our society which, despite its highly-organized leisure-time provisions, is terribly empty: unaesthetic, unmusical, ungifted for the religious dimension, with no taste for the good news coming from God and leading to him, no sense for an enthusiastic faith or for gratitude and praise to God.

God did not create and redeem his world for mere consumption and production. Utility is not the last word on men and women and the creation entrusted to them. Our biblical religion implies marvelling, admiring, joy, thanksgiving, praise. To rejoice in whatever is beautiful, despite all the dilemmas of utility, is a wonderful act of gratitude to God.

According to St Thomas Aquinas, beauty is one of the most characteristic names of God. Creation and redemption are revelation of his glory, splendour of his own beauty. The vision in the Book of Revelation quoted at the beginning of this chapter is an essential feature of God's promises. It presumes the sense for beauty.

Beauty speaks to us in our wholeness; it is attractive beyond all considerations of utility and profit. Loving people — beautiful and attractive themselves — discover the beauty, the goodness, the authenticity of others. They see the others' inner resources and awaken them. Openness to beauty unfolds in contemplation and is the most cheerful pathway to all that is good and true. Indeed, beauty itself is the splendour of what is true and good.

Whoever has developed a sense for authentic beauty cannot be seduced by cheap sex-appeal but has an open eye for people who beautifully radiate truthfulness, kindness, serenity, peace. One senses that these people are of themselves an invitation to strive for goodness and authenticity.

In its enchanting purity and integrity, beauty speaks to the believer in an inner language that sings of the glory of a loving Creator who, in all his works, reveals his own beauty and generosity. St Augustine expresses a primordial religious experience of millions of people when he prays: "How beautiful is everything which you have made! But how ineffably more beautiful are you, the Creator of all things!"

The Holy Spirit is called not only the 'Spirit of Truth' but also the 'glorious Spirit' (cf. 1 Pet 4:14). Whoever is guided by the Spirit in a life of constant gratitude and grateful service is led to an ever deeper and more beatifying knowledge of the 'Father of glory', the 'Lord of glory and majesty.'

The word 'glory' is a key word in the holy scriptures. Religious people speak of glory when they are wholly seized by God's attractive and awe-inspiring majesty, filled with joy by his nearness and love and at the same time by a loving fear in the face of his holiness.

This basic experience of holy fear, of awe, marvel and bliss, gives to the Christian the strength to follow Christ Crucified, in view of "the revelation of the glory of God in the face of Jesus Christ", for Jesus "caused his light to shine within us" (2 Cor 4:6).

When he is ready to drink the bitter chalice and to accept the outrage of the cross, Jesus prays to the Father: "The glory which thou gavest me I have given to them, that they may be one, as we are one . . . Father, I desire that these men, who are thy gift to me, may be with me where I am; so that they may look upon my glory, which thou has given me because thou didst love me before the world began" (Jn 17:22–24). A Christian cannot think about eternal beatitude without constantly praising God's glory and majesty, his attractive and awe-inspiring beauty whose blissful and resplendent rays already light the faces of saints.

The biblical morality of the beatitudes is one of beauty and glory, infinitely more fruitful and attractive than a mere morality of duties and prohibitions. Those who develop the sense of beauty gain a better access and a more grateful relationship to the whole of reality. Experiencing the beauty and bounty of God's good world, they open themselves wholly to a morality of grace and graciousness. They sense then the depth of the words of St Paul: "You are no longer under law, but under the grace of God" (Rom 6:14).

An inner relationship with beauty, in view of him who *is*

Beauty, gives to the christian life a note of joy, courage and creativity. Beauty itself is a gratuitous gift. It does not cry out, 'do this, do that', but it transforms the human mind and heart, intuition, spirit and will. It forms a personality whose relationship with the realm of the good, the honest, the fitting and the truth is connatural: a christian person who finds his or her joy in God.

This is shown in the lives of the saints. We think of the joy of St Francis of Assisi in whatever is beautiful, especially the simple and ordinary things. This allowed him a kind of espousal with 'Lady Poverty' in a constant festival of joy. Or we think of St Alphonsus, so enraptured by the beauty of divine love and glory, that in the midst of a sermon he could compose songs and sing the good news into the hearts of the faithful: songs which for hundreds of years re-echoed his enthusiasm for the Emmanuel — God with us. Some of his spiritual works, for instance, *The Art of Loving Jesus Christ* awakened enthusiasm in thousands of readers.

So now, as always, the world needs saints who will educate children, youth and adults in a sense of beauty as radiance of the good and the true. This is an absolute necessity if we want to help our culture to rise above an insensitive, sterile, consumer-producer mentality. Such an advance would also do much for the liberation of our society from the ugliness of aggressiveness and violence.

Everyone is meant by God to become a masterpiece of his love and, at the same time, his coartist in his wonderful work of forming human beings in his authentic image. Everyone can develop some dimension of art, of creativity. But whatever our individual skills or limits in human arts, we can become masters in the supreme art of being loving and lovable people; indeed, of becoming saints and helping each other in this most wonderful art. We have the divine promises. The world does not need humans as mass-produced products, producers or consumers. It needs beautiful, whole and holy people.

*   *   *

Father of glory and majesty, we praise you for all the beauty of your creation: the bright firmament, the green of our meadows, the quiet and healthy air of the forests, the gaiety and splendour of flowers, the love songs of birds and the ever new beauty of thousands of species of animals. Wherever we look, we see the reflection of your own beauty, inviting us to marvel, to admire, to praise and to thank you.

We praise you for each smile of a beloved child, for the radiant faces of true lovers, for the hope-inspiring beauty of mature kindliness in so many people, for the magnificence of the wholeness of holy people.

We praise you for your wonders in the history of salvation, for the Book of Psalms and all the holy scriptures, which teach us to discover better and better the beauty of all your works and the admirable wisdom revealed in the work of redemption.

Above all, we praise you for the great miracle of the incarnation of your beloved Son, Jesus Christ, for his attractive kindness to all who came to him, for the majesty of his forgiveness and love on the cross, for the revelation of your glory in his resurrection, and for the promise of our resurrection in glory if our life here on earth glorifies your majesty and love.

Lord, teach us to marvel, to admire, to praise and thank you for your beauty and the beauty of all your creation.

CHAPTER FOUR

Feast and leisure

"I rejoiced when they said to me,
'Let us go to the house of the Lord.'
Now we stand within your gates, O Jerusalem:
Jerusalem that is built to be a city
where people come together in unity;
to which the tribes resort, the tribes of the Lord,
to give thanks to the Lord himself,
the bounden duty of Israel.
For in her are set the thrones of justice,
the thrones of the house of David.
Pray for the peace of Jerusalem:
'May those who love you prosper;
peace be within your ramparts
and prosperity in your palaces.'
For the sake of these my brothers and my friends,
I will say, 'Peace be within you.'
For the sake of the house of the Lord our God
I will pray for your good" (Ps 122).

FREQUENTLY I have heard the following definition of the difference between the typical German and the typical Italian: "the German lives to work; the Italian works to live." If this is true, the Italian is winning the match — provided, however, that he knows the art of living.

The ultimate sense of life is not in work and not in play. A fulfilled life implies both meaningful leisure and honourable, socially-relevant work. In biblical religion life is, above all, a feast spreading its meaning and joy over all of life's dimensions.

Jesus has not only borne our burdens and laboured on the cross; we know him equally as the one who has concelebrated the feasts of Israel, as the one who has sung the joyful songs of the pilgrims on their way to the house of God. He exulted in his work and his praise of his Father. These were his resources which made him strong for his way of the cross. Before he went

29

up to the Mount of Olives and to Mount Calvary, he instituted the Eucharist which anticipates and guides us to the heavenly banquet of eternal bliss.

Being a Christian surely requires the readiness to follow Christ, the Crucified, but it means also that we are set free for joyous festival, dancing before the Lord, quiet contemplation, raptures of love, conviviality, laughter and a liberating sense of humour.

Feast and leisure are a relaxed but firm 'Yes' to life's meaning, an occasion for sharing life's joys, strengthening solidarity in joy and sorrow, developing creativity. All this has great impact on our personal growth, creative liberty and fidelity.

If we celebrate feasts and make our life festive in expectation of the eternal feast, then we know that it is good to live, that it is wonderful to live together, that life has an ultimate purpose surpassing all the purposes of work and organization. We have all the reasons for contemplation and celebration. We are constantly invited to rejoice in all that is good, true and beautiful, and we know that our origin is in him who is love, goodness, truth, bliss.

Quite different are the feasts and leisure times of people driven by the anguish of not being able to amass enough. The prophet gives us their sad picture: "Let us eat and drink; for tomorrow we die" (Is 22:13). They need the loudest rock music, louder than the noise of our streets and louder than the cry of their hearts which yearn for ultimate meaning, true love and joy. They want to deafen themselves to their inner voice that calls for conversion.

Even more deplorable are the 'festivals' of the dictators of ideologies who talk of class struggle and liberation while, by their lust for power, their deadly bureaucracy and their murderous arms race, they have already buried even the false hopes of the original ideology. So they feast on the great parades of their newest weaponry and the applause of their propagandized masses.

Leisure, feast, celebration, play and dance mean more than repose from work and restoration of strength for work. They bear meaning in themselves for all who are searching for life's final meaning. They are gateways to new horizons.

The book of Genesis helps us to discover the meaning of

the sabbath in view of the supreme dignity of man, created in God's own image. The seventh day should remind God's people not only of the Creator's works but also of his repose, his celebration of love and joy, over and above all his works (cf. Gen 1 : 27; 2 : 1–4).

God does not want man to be a drudge, a slave of work. The sacred days guaranteeing repose and leisure should help us to develop our noblest capacities for adoration, for joy and love. Only thus can we be faithful and creative stewards of the earth entrusted to us. We cannot be truthfully an image and likeness of God in our work unless we are his image, above all, in the joy of feast that calls for love and unity.

Jesus insists that the sabbath is for man (cf. Mk 2 : 27). It is a privilege, an invitation to a supreme sharing in God's feast and peace, it is also a fundamental social legislation to protect servants, migrants, slaves (cf. Ex 20 : 10). It reminds everyone that, before God, the poor and oppressed are of the same dignity as the rich and powerful, and that nobody may celebrate the feast of liberation wrought by God if he or she refuses to the weaker ones a share in the benefits. The world — economic, cultural, social and political — needs saints who celebrate life in this way, as feast to which all others are invited.

Our christian life is marked by the year's liturgical cycle. The feasts of the year and the christian Sunday offer a sharing in salvation history through grateful remembrance of God's wonderful deeds of creation and redemption, the expectation of an eternal sharing in God's glory and bliss, and the ongoing discovery of present opportunities.

Feast and leisure do not lull the Christian to sleep or to forgetfulness of injustice and misery in the world. Rather, those who truthfully celebrate the feasts of salvation find enough energy not only to deal with their own troubles but also to bear the burdens of each other. They know well that only thus are we all together on the road to the common feast of eternal life.

The Eucharist, sacrifice and banquet, memorial and pledge of abiding hope, opens our eyes to the abyss of sin in the light of Christ's cross, but also assures us of the final victory of justice and love. Our celebration of the remembrance and hope of liberation, and of the presence of him who is the Helper of the poor, is honest and fruitful only if we are joined in the struggle for the dignity and liberty of all people.

Some seem to think that their serious commitment to social and political action allows or even bids them to turn away from feast and adoration. They have gone astray. They deny themselves the very inner resources of peace, without which they cannot order a halt to discord, hatred or injustice. If we refuse to take time to adore God together and to open ourselves to his gospel, we lose our chance to exorcise the false gods from our own hearts and the dangerous idols from public life.

The order of christian feasts, combined with the regularity of the Sunday remembrance of the events of the history of salvation — especially the Easter event — is a wonderful gift of the Lord of salvation history. It is also a pedagogical masterpiece. Humankind would not be so restless and unstable if it would thankfully accept this divine pedagogy. Not all the sports and sport reviews, movies and entertainments of the leisure industries will fill the void in the souls and lives of those who reject the rhythm of the christian feasts and Sundays; they become only new seductions for estrangement.

This does not imply that the feasts and celebrations of the church claim a kind of monopoly. But their centrality touches on all the joys and sorrows of life, yet leaves room for the myriad forms of festivity and recreation. And everything that is genuine in the feasts and joys of families, neighbourhoods, cultures, can be a kind of prelude to the religious celebrations.

The saint is never a killjoy. The dimension of dance and play is indispensable in human culture. The child needs play, playmates and joy in play. Parents who play with their children reap their own joyous harvest of serenity. Delight in play and a sense for the rules of fair play repel a too heavy seriousness and prepare for fair cooperation in life's tasks and teamwork.

As if in an enchanting playlet, holy scripture tells us of the working of divine wisdom and of the invitation to the feast which divine wisdom prepares for those whom she loves (cf. Prov 9: 1–6). And divine wisdom tells us: "Then I was at his side each day, his darling and delight, playing in his presence continually, playing on the earth, when he had finished it, while my delight was in mankind" (Prov 8: 30–31). On the way to the eternal feast in the glory of God, we are team players, 'members of the cast' in the tremendous play of redemption, of the gradual breakthrough of joy and love.

To be sure, we also need purposefulness in our life, a prudent coordination of means (tools and methods) and intentions. But purposes and tools must not be allowed to dominate us. God offers us many joys without subordinating them in any way to direct purposes. Let us, time and again, accept the invitation simply to rejoice, to sing and to play!

The self-portrayal of man in various kinds of art is an echo of God's rejoicing in his creation and redemption. If someone objects, "But we are far from being simply redeemed", then my suggestion is, "Therefore, there is even a greater need for play therapy, the joy of team play, for wit and laughter." The Christian who knows that he is redeemed can laugh in spite of all his shadows, in spite of all the misery, for he believes that the last word in history is the victory of love and joy.

Not all Christians, not even all saints, are especially gifted with a sense of humour; but no saint will ever disdain this wonderful gift. It is, indeed, a precious charism that often provides admirable skill in disentangling mixed proportions and opening people's eyes for a balanced vision of events.

It can be a marvellous peace-making charism. As Christians we know about the crooked lines of our sinful earth, about foolishness and sin. But we also know that, after all, redemption is plentiful and victorious. So we allow ourselves and others a portion of foolishness while constantly striving for greater wisdom.

A genuine and healthy sense of humour never focusses on other peoples' errors or failures. The tone and target of a redeemed Christian's humour reveal his constant awareness that he, too, has his share of foolishness and shadows, and that he is in the same boat with the others to whom the play therapy of his humour is directed.

Christian humour has its roots in the knowledge that, in spite of our sins and shortcomings, we are accepted and reconciled by God. The 'Yes' to the provisional arises from a firm hope in final salvation. A purifying and reconciling sense of humour is a concrete sign and symbol of faith that conquers the hearts of many: not a superficial or blind optimism but the experience of God's graciousness which allows us to discover a reason

C

for wit and laughter where others see only doom. It signals hope and redeemed freedom.

∗   ∗   ∗

We thank you, Father, that on our pilgrimage you grant us not only time to rest after all the toil but also festive joy and leisure for contemplation. Like children, we can play before you, confident that it pleases you to see us bring happiness to each other in good team play and common celebration.

We thank you for the great feasts of the church in which we can experience salvation solidarity and shared joy. Through them you remind us of the past salvation history and direct our eyes and steps towards the eternal homeland. You help us, too, to discover the richness of the present moment, reassuring us of your abiding presence and loving care.

I thank you for the yearly remembrance of my birthday and day of baptism. You have called me into being, given me a unique name and have assumed me into the family of the redeemed.

I thank you for all our family's feasts and celebrations, for play and song with brothers and sisters, for the time our parents took to play and to talk with us.

Thank you, Father, for the wonderful people who, through wit and humour, have helped us to see redemption at work and to discover essential dimensions of life, of beauty, of inner liberty and creativity.

Grant that, for all of us, feast, dance and play, song and sense of humour may be part of our grateful experience of redemption at work.

Free the world from that brutish seriousness and cold calculation which often lead to tensions and war. Send saints to the world to announce to it the rays of liberation!

CHAPTER FIVE

The mass media

"The heavens tell out the glory of God,
the vault of heaven reveals his handiwork.
One day speaks to another,
night with night shares its knowledge,
and this without speech or language
or sound of any voice.
Their music goes out through all the earth,
their words reach to the end of the world" (Ps 19:1–4).

"There is nothing covered up that will not be uncovered,
nothing hidden that will not be made known. What I say
to you in the dark you must repeat in broad daylight; what
you hear whispered you must shout from the house" (Mt
10:26–27).

FEW things challenge the Christian's discernment and competence as much as the modern mass-media. If Christians who excel
in this field can bring to it strong convictions, the art of dialogue,
vigilance for the signs of the times, and discernment, then they
belong to those saints of whom the world is most in need.

Today's mass media offer a unique opportunity for proclaiming the good news literally 'from the housetops' — think of all
those TV aerials! The potential of the various forms of news,
information and entertainment media is stupendous. They can
contribute to conscience-raising about the urgent problems of our
times, spread peace-fostering information, give voice to the voice-
less, awaken people's consciences to the plight of the hungry, the
exploited, the victims of catastrophies, and be instruments for
organizing actions of solidarity from one end of the earth to the
other.

On the other hand, there is nothing more dangerous than
the same mass media if they are in the hands of the conscience-
less, the inculcators of ideologies or exploiters of human passion,
greed and aggressiveness. The infatuation of a great part of the

German population with Hitler can exemplify this, for it could hardly have been possible without a shrewd use of the radio to propagandize a people not yet prepared for discernment in its use.

When Hitler came to power, each family was offered a receiver at almost no cost. My own father's reaction was sharp: "As long as this man is in power, no receiver will come into our house; I don't want this voice heard in our home!" A neighbouring family, as devout and church-oriented as ours, took the receiver. After a few years they had not, thanks be to God, lost their faith, but their trust in church leaders was undermined, and many of Hitler's slogans had taken over a good part of their thinking and their language.

Some years later, I found in homes in Russian cities a radio loudspeaker which could neither be turned off nor be tuned into any other programme. It had been designed by the inculcators of Stalinism. Both of these régimes threatened grave sanctions against anyone who dared to listen to another country's radio or ideology.

Development of the mass media has brought and is still bringing forth profound cultural and psychological changes. Here is a field where Christians have to be present in many ways: not only through some religious programmes but in all areas, especially the cultural and entertainment fields. We have to be well informed about how the mass media shape human consciousness; and we have to learn how to use them, avoiding every kind of manipulation of people's minds, and fostering the virtues of critique (discernment), creative liberty and constructive action.

Anyone who wants to develop his or her humanness and to have a share in the use of these media and the various possibilities to influence them has to be critical about his or her own reactions and cultivate intensively the virtue of discernment.

When letterpress printing appeared five hundred years ago and won a growing influence on public opinion, the church reacted one-sidedly by all available means of control, censure and sanctions. The Index of forbidden books was one of its measures. This was understandable, since the public was in no way prepared for the necessary discernment. Of course, this kind of repressive control over the modern mass media (radio, movies, TV) is absolutely impossible now, and the reaction of most people is against a negative control system. But responsible users of the media can praise good programmes, recommend certain movies and plays, and warn against error and decadence. But it can happen that loud condemnation and warnings by church authorities can boomerang and sometimes make an otherwise unsuccessful book, movie or play a money-maker.

What really matters today is that each individual, family, group and community tries to grow in discernment and to foster discernment in church and society. The person-to-person propaganda in favour of good books, periodicals, movies, TV programmes and the like is a very effective means of promoting the good and increasing one's own competence in discernment. Shared efforts in such critique are especially effective.

In this field, too, we remember one of the basic christian and human principles: to give prime attention to discovering and promoting the good. Then we can also more systematically and effectively face the evil, unmask deceptions and hazards, and warn against them.

Modern mass media offer a thoroughly new chance to give to all social classes and all nations easier access to the common cultural patrimony. But a concerted effort is needed to guarantee a certain moral and cultural level, to check the efforts of power cliques to use the media abusively, and to block effectively any kind of group monopoly. Here is one of the most important fields for lay apostolate and professional excellence.

A serious danger is passive receptivity, exposing oneself uncritically to a chaotic flow of news and entertainment without asking what good or harm they bring, how credible and how relevant they are and what kind of action they provoke. Another danger is the exaggerated star-cult in literary and entertainment fields and even in the sports world, which frequently leads to the imitation of those who least deserve it. Many people tend to accept opinions uncritically simply because they are uttered by their favourite stars.

The media customer should, if competent, be active in many ways. Active insertion into the dialogue allows one to exercise a beneficial influence on public opinion instead of exposing oneself defencelessly to all kinds of dubious influences.

The most accessible means of influence is a critical choice of the products of the press, films, cassettes, radio and TV programmes, by which the client says his mighty word through the market. Another important means is by letter, to the editor, journalist or artist, especially if one's opinion is expressed competently and constructively. It is not fitting, however, to send only letters of censure and reproach. The eternal quarreler quickly loses any chance of being listened to or taken seriously. Positive appraisal, however, can be very effective.

The director of a broadcasting company once told me that good programmes, good music, good entertainment frequently have little chance because nobody requests them and nobody praises them. Many years ago, when I was still teaching in our scholasticate in Germany, I was visited by a friend of a famous entertainer who had died few days before. He had come to bring to our students the entertainer's greetings uttered on his deathbed. Some weeks previously they had written a collective letter to him, praising the synthesis of his good taste, competence and decency. His reaction had been one of great joy, but also occasioned the remark: "During so many years of my career I never received any acknowledgement from any churchman; yet what these students of theology have praised in my work was my most serious concern during my whole life".

Families should pay serious attention to their choice of TV programmes. They are inviting guests into their home and recommending them to their children. The adults, adolescents and children in a family should get together frequently in a common effort to choose good programmes. If first they discuss the criteria and then exchange their evaluations after having watched the programmes, they will be sure that they, and not their TV guests, are the ones who have the last word in their home. But in many families, unfortunately, the art of dialogue and even common family prayer have been silenced by the craving for ever new programmes which are received uncritically and passively.

The consumer of mass media products needs to practise many forms of asceticism. It is not sufficient to protect oneself against bad and poisonous quality; quantity, too, has to be watched: how much time? How many useless impressions and reactions? How much money? How much passivity in children?

Anyone who realizes how much the audio-visual media influence and change our psychic life needs no further warning. But those who continue to consume too much and too passively will become addicted consumers unable to digest the material. Such people gradually lose the contemplative dimension of life. The art of dialogue becomes even more difficult and more rare.

Years ago I was invited by a group of major superiors to a study week on the problems of chastity in religious life. Also present were some outstanding psychologists and psycho-therapists. I was amazed when I heard a well-known psychologist from Harvard University, the mother of several children, suggest to the superiors that they advise their confreres to allow themselves a longer period — perhaps a year — of complete abstinence from TV and movies, and then to assess their first reactions when viewing again what they had earlier watched so often. She also pointed to the fact that, both on TV and in magazines, sexuality frequently is presented in the context of incitement to many forms of consumerism, with the result that the passive receiver of these messages gradually becomes used to the idea that sexuality is just another consumer good.

This leads us to another dimension of a much-needed asceticism for those who allow themselves to be exposed too often to TV publicity and advertisements. The 'new commandments' are inculcated there: "Thou shalt covet, thou shalt buy more things; thou shalt parade thy needs and means, consume more . . .". We have to be on guard against these 'hidden seducers'.

Particularly dangerous is the intensive advertising for psycho-tropic drugs. By word and picture the uncritical watcher is lulled into the belief that almost every troublesome emotion, stress and pain can be relieved by taking the recommended drug. Drug addiction in our society is only the tip of the iceberg of an ever-growing tendency, propagated by the drug industry, to swallow psychotropic pills instead of discovering and organizing one's own spiritual and psychological resources, living within one's capacities and caring for healthier relationships with one's family, neighbours and community.

Through the modern mass media, almost everyone today is either exposed passively to or meets critically the pluralism of cultures and world views. The era of closed groups and cultures has ended. People are guided no longer by uniform tradi-ditions, customs, mores, world views, convictions. The media allow us to compare the great diversity in all these dimensions.

This can be accepted as a challenge to search more thoroughly for truth and solid convictions of conscience, and thereby to sink deeper roots into the community of faith. There one finds the most valid help, especially when it fosters careful discernment and distinction between the abiding truth of divine revelation on the one hand and, on the other, changing human traditions and world views.

The need for mature discernment is heightened by the fact that today's pluralism not only issues an invitation to constructive dialogue and peaceful competition but is open to intolerant and aggressive ideologies as well, not to mention economic and political systems whose weaponry is the ruthless manipulation of people's minds.

Many Christians, unfortunately, are not prepared to confront the complex problem of pluralism critically and constructively. We all should help one another to hold firmly to the abiding truths and principles of our faith and to unmask dangerous errors, while at the same time being open-minded to a great diversity of life expressions, which can be vital incarnations of the one faith in various times and cultures. For this, too, the world needs saints: mature and competent Christians.

The way Christians are present in the world of the mass media decides very much the influence they will bring to bear on the burning questions of our day and our world, such as the reconciliation of the christian churches and reconciliation and peace among nations.

*   *   *

God, our Father, we adore you for the wonders of your communication. We thank you for Christ, the great communicator on earth. We praise you for sending us the Spirit of Truth, enabling us to become mindful recipients and skilful and respectful communicators of truth.

We praise you, God, for having enabled men and women to discover more and more the secrets hidden in your creation, allowing them new forms of communication by wireless radio-telegraphy, television and new systems of satellites, so that news can go from one end of the earth to the other in seconds. Progress in research tells us of ever new dimensions of the greatness of your creation.

Father, we do believe that it is your design to lead us all to you through your communication in creation and redemption. We thank you for the mass media, through which you invite the whole of humanity to a worldwide dialogue, new forms of solidarity, and new means of fostering peace. Help us, Lord, to reach that level of wisdom and discernment that allows us to make beneficial use of all these means.

CHAPTER SIX

Shared responsibility for healthy public opinions

"Shame on you! you who drag wickedness along like a tethered sheep, and sin like a heifer on a rope . . . Shame on you! you who call evil good and good evil, who turn darkness into light and light into darkness, who make bitter sweet and sweet bitter. Shame on you! you who are wise in your own eyes and prudent in your own esteem" (Is 5: 18–21).

SINCE christian holiness means essentially mission to be 'light to the world', it is unthinkable that a genuine Christian would ignore or neglect a proper share of responsibility for the formation of healthy public opinions in his or her immediate environment and in society at large. The common effort to illumine public opinion is a basic function of our care for the common good.

I am not speaking here of merely theoretical opinions which have no relevance to life, love and justice in human relationships. What I have in mind are those convictions and opinions which shape the human milieu, human encounter and cooperation, individual and collective responsibility.

Examples will explain what we are about. Public opinion on one burning issue of the day can say, "Life is something wonderful, a sign of God's creative presence. Human life, from the very beginning, is entrusted to the responsibility and protection of all. If society and state do not protect the life of the weakest and most innocent ones, the common good is shaken at its very foundations." But in some circles public opinion sounds like this: "My womb is mine. Therefore it matters to nobody else if I interrupt an unwanted pregnancy."

In the economic realm, one trend of public opinion tells

us by words and practice: "What counts in the national economy is the quantitative growth of output. If a government fails on this item, it should have no further chance." Yet I am convinced that I should influence public opinion in a quite different direction, since I believe that the striving for ever more output and the tendency to measure prosperity and the common good by the quantitative national gross product are grievous errors with disastrous consequences for the future and dignity of humankind. The mania for quantitative growth can gravely harm the true (holistic) growth of persons and communities. If we do not liberate ourselves from this 'more, more', 'bigger, bigger' madness, then sooner or later it will lead to the fight of all against all, and even to an ecological collapse.

A third example is equally vital. One trend concentrates the question of human health on the right of health care for all. "The state and society have to do much more for health, and I have the right to get as much as possible from them and from the insurance fund." But again I choose to think differently. Surely the common good and justice require our state and society (us!) to provide the best possible care for the sick, the handicapped and the poor. But the main efforts in public health should be directed towards eliminating the common causes of sickness and handicap: all forms of addiction that cripple persons, personalities and human relationships. People have to be more sensitized to their own responsibility for their health and that of others. They should appreciate and use their own inner resources and help others to do so. We owe it to ourselves, our families and the common good to promote health by a healthy life-style.

One can conjure up a dozen other examples to show that the shape of public opinions decides what will be done in matters of justice, the quality of life, and peace. Almost all the great decisions in the life of individuals, families and nations are programmed and somehow predestined by the quality of reigning public opinions. This is especially true in an era of democracy.

Those who are neglecting their commitment to the formation of good public opinion are wrong when, at the same time, they request that those in authority pass laws and enforce measures which are clearly contradicted by a public-opinion majority. If the government were to yield to the pressure of a minority which has failed to make the proper contribution towards forming a consenting public opinion, then the government would be voted out in the next election. Meanwhile it would have had little success with measures that found no genuine echo in the forum of public opinion.

However, it should not be overlooked that legislation and provisions taken by administrators are also factors influencing public opinions, particularly if the legislators and administrators can give convincing reasons for their decisions. For them, too, the art of dialogue and an intelligent contribution to public opinion are decisive. But all citizens should see in this field their great chance for decisive action.

The right to free public utterance of opinions and convictions, and to active participation in efforts to form public opinion, is a modern acquisition. Right-wing dictators, as well as the communist bureaucracy, deny and oppose this right. Citizens in their countries have only the right to applaud the measures and ideologies of the powerful. Transgressions are not only severely punished, but the moralism of the power cliques imposes heavy moral charges against opponents.

In healthy democracies the right to free expression has its limits. It cannot be allowed when the evident intention is the elimination of democracy, especially by violent means, or oppression of the majority, or public incitement to crimes against others. As Christians, we say a firm 'Yes' to freedom of expression within the indicated limits. This 'Yes' has two presuppositions: the first is that we are willing to accept our shared responsibility in the search for healthy public opinions and to acquire the necessary competence for that purpose; the second is that we tirelessly seek after truth and justice.

Historically, the presupposition for the public right to free expression and for diffusion of opinions is grounded in the victory over an arrogant élitism. Secular and ecclesiastical circles opposed freedom of public expression because of a deeply-rooted pessimism about the good will and wisdom of the simple people, the 'masses', combined with a naïve optimism about their own capacity to know what is right, true and good. The Roman poet, Ovid, expressed this mentality with the well-known words, "Odi profanum vulgus et arceo" (I hate the profane masses and keep them at a distance). History provides enough evidence to show that the hidden reason why powerful minorities excluded the large majorities from the process of searching for truth and from decision-making was simply the selfish group's interest and lust for power.

Already, in the latter part of the last century, Pope Leo XIII spoke clearly about freedom of public utterance of opinions and convictions within the church. "In questions on which God or the church has not spoken a final word, in questions which God has left to free expression, everybody may think as he likes; and he may utter what he thinks is right. This is not against natural law. This freedom will not seduce men, or oppress truth, but rather in numerous cases will help to find truth and to bring it into full light." Pius XII later insisted that the right to participate in the process of forming public opinions belongs to the faithful within the church as much as within secular society.

The teaching authorities in the church have a particular duty to be a learning church. Listening to the word of God and proclaiming it cannot be disassociated from listening to people, especially to those of humble condition, of whom Jesus speaks in a jubilant prayer: "I thank thee, Father, Lord of heaven and earth, for hiding these things from the learned and wise, and revealing them to the simple. Yes, Father, such was thy choice" (Lk 10:21). The background is that in Jesus' time, the religious rulers and the ruling class showed great contempt for the lower social classes, especially for the rural population. But most of the prophets came from those parts of the nation.

The Second Vatican Council says explicitly that lay people, too, participate in the prophetic mission of the church. And it draws some important conclusions, such as: "An individual layman, by reason of the knowledge, competence, or outstanding ability which he may enjoy, is permitted and sometimes even obliged to express his opinion on things which concern the good of the church" (*The Church*, 37).

Even in matters of doctrine which allow no contradiction, not only ordained theologians but also lay people can make relevant contributions towards formulating these truths in a way that manifests their fruitfulness for life and makes them more understandable for the various cultures and social classes.

In all questions to which there is no definite response from divine revelation, the whole people of God actively participate in the effort to find the proper judgements and solutions. The stream of information and competent knowledge — although not that of 'competence of office' — flows in from all directions.

On decisions about concrete, historically-conditioned problems which require a knowledge of life as much as of general principles, no authority has the right to renounce the contributions of those who have a special competence and valuable experience. For example, we can cite the long debates about charging a moderate interest on capital loans ('usury'). For centuries, the Magisterium simply reaffirmed earlier formulations and definitions, while lay people and theologians, although agreeing with the general principles which condemned usury, pointed to the different situation in modern economy. A deeper understanding of the role of interest under the new situation also helped to provide more convincing arguments against the sins of usury and exploitation. By not accepting the input from lay people and theologians, the representatives of the authoritative Magisterium caused great losses and suffering, and also harmed their credibility in this and in other matters.

Our sense of responsibility for searching out and propagating sound opinions goes hand in hand with a sharper awareness of the limits of our competence. If the subject matter concerns vital problems and interests, this does not mean that those who have no outstanding competence have to be silent. Rather, all should be learners in order to improve competence. The best way usually is by dialogue. Thereby we learn carefully to distinguish between deeply-rooted and matured convictions on the one hand and, on the other, tentative opinions. Sometimes our best contribution is a well-formulated question rather than a daring thesis. The formulation and further discussion of the proper questions will induce all participants to more serious reflection, including those who propose the questions.

In the propagation of public opinions, Christians will think not in terms of overcoming the others and being the victors, but simply of making their creative contribution in the search for truth and truthful solutions to vital problems. Those whose first impulse is to impose their opinions on others will not refrain from manipulation or abusive measures. Manipulation operates with a shrewd mixture of praise and blame, remuneration and threat, and uses all kinds of deceptive manoeuvres. One of its most effective tools is semantics.

Authentic cooperation in searching out and propagating sound public opinions implies a dialogue and reciprocity of consciences dedicated to truth and goodness. "In fidelity to conscience Christians are joined with the rest of men in the search for truth and for the genuine solution to the numerous problems which arise both in the life of individuals and from social relationships" (*The Church in the Modern World*, 16).

Only in love and responsibility for the common good, for the well-being of our neighbours, and in absolute respect for every sincere conscience, can we fulfil our role in this fundamental area. And I would like to add that only by developing our contemplative dimension in the light of God, Father of all, can we avoid the danger of becoming manipulated manipulators.

*   *   *

Lord Jesus Christ, you tell us poor sinners that we are 'light for the world'. Let us never forget that you alone can say, 'I am the light of the world'. We can receive your light and the mission to be light for others only as a gratuitous gift from you. Help us to abide and to walk in your light so that we may discern everything in the light of your love and truth.

Lord, we live in an ambiguous world which can easily seduce us unless we have made a firm option to follow your light, an option which has to be more and more consolidated in our whole being. Lord, cleanse us, strengthen us, so that we may become more and more transparent and your light can shine through us. Make us a radiant community of faith, hope and love, zealous for your saving justice.

Help us to create a 'divine milieu' around us, to operate effectively for public opinions which favour justice, reconciliation and peace, truthfulness and sobriety. Confirm our purpose to acquire that purity of motives and that competence which will allow us to exercise a healing influence on public life through good public opinions.

CHAPTER SEVEN

Marked by faith

"Take up God's armour; then you will be able to stand your ground when things are at their worst, to complete every task and still to stand. Stand firm I say. Fasten on the belt of truth; for coat of mail put on integrity; let the shoes on your feet be the gospel of peace, to give you firm footing; and with all these, take up the great shield of faith, with which you will be able to quench all the flaming arrows of the evil one. Take salvation for helmet; for sword, take that which the Spirit gives you — the words that come from God" (Eph 6 : 13–17).

"I count everything sheer loss, because all is far out-weighed by the gain of knowing Christ Jesus my Lord . . . and finding myself incorporate in him, with no righteousness of my own, no legal rectitude, but the righteousness which comes from faith in Christ, given by God in response to faith. All I care for is to know Christ, to experience the power of his resurrection, and to share his sufferings, in growing conformity with his death, if only I may finally arrive at the resurrection from the dead" (Phil 3 : 8–11).

CHRISTIANS have their identity and the radiance of their witness and service by faith. In faith they recognize that everything comes from God, the Father of all. Gratitude for the gift of faith and the joy that arises from faith dedicate them to the service of the gospel. Experiencing in faith the power of God's grace, they know that the world needs, above all else, a share in this gift.

The 'shield of faith' is not meant for mere self-defence; this most precious gift gives them 'firm footing' while bringing 'the gospel of peace' to humankind. The 'helmet of salvation' is linked with the 'sword which the Spirit gives' — 'the word of God'. This is what the world needs most. God's people sharing the light, joy and strength of faith with as many people as possible, in gratitude for the gift of faith and joy which the Spirit gives. Saints are marked by the death of Christ and live in conformity with it; but equally they are people who experience 'the power of the resurrection'.

The 'Yes' of faith is essentially a grateful 'Yes' to the gift of faith, and a readiness to walk on its road in the community of faith. On the universal vocation to holiness, the Second Vatican Council says: "Every person should walk unhesitatingly according to his own personal gifts and duties in the path of a living faith which arouses hopes and works through charity" (*The Church*, 41).

Speaking on faith we must know what we mean. A parish priest in Rome sent an engaged couple to me. He had refused to perform a wedding ceremony for them in church because he considered them unbelievers who wanted the ceremony only for the sake of their relatives. They protested that they were believers. The man said, "I believe in Jesus of Nazareth; he was one of the greatest forerunners of Karl Marx and Mao tse Tung." The woman said, "I do believe in some supreme being." But for us, faith is not something confused and arbitrary. It has a clear content, the whole of God's revelation. We believe in the living God who has revealed himself in Jesus Christ.

Aristotle and other philosophers proved that there must be a prime cause setting all other causes in movement. This is not false, but inasmuch as nothing is said about the God who is Love it is a far cry from what we believe.

Deeply touched by the insight that christian faith is infinitely more wonderful than the insights of the philosophers, Blaise Pascal wrote with his own blood his confession of faith in the God of history: ". . . not the god of the philosophers, but the God of Abraham, the God of Isaac, the God of Jacob, the God and Father of our Lord Jesus Christ." Our confession of faith is praise of God arising from our innermost self. It is the life-response to the One who is 'God-with-us', who calls us to an intimate communion. In faith we entrust ourselves to God, accept wholeheartedly our marvellous vocation, and dedicate ourselves to God's kingdom.

Faith which grants salvation is the great feast of love and trust. In the Old Testament God revealed himself as 'spouse' of Israel. In Jesus Christ the Godhead has espoused humanity

49

D

forever in an indissoluble covenant between God and humankind. In Jesus Christ God tells us irrevocably that he enters into communion with us, that his love and mercy is without end, that he calls us to be his holy people, and that he has prepared for us an endless feast in an unsurpassable sharing in his triune love.

In faith everyone responds with his or her unique name but no one can forget that God wants all people to share in his revelation and life. Faith-experience is essentially a mission and inner dynamic to share the joy of faith and to give witness to its content and joy as much as possible.

In faith I rejoice in being loved by him who is Love. But in faith I rejoice equally in knowing that all are loved by God and invited to his feast of love. In faith I can marvel, wonder, adore. And what does the world of today need more than this? I cannot imagine an authentic believer who does not have a strong desire, a yearning that all people may come to the same joy and strength of faith. So it is natural that Paul, in his eulogy on faith, should invite believers to "give yourselves wholly to prayer and entreaty; pray on every occasion in the power of the Spirit . . . always interceding for all God's people" (Eph 6:18).

An essential dimension of christian faith is the joyful celebration of the sacraments of faith in the festive community. Faith wants sharing, singing, experience of solidarity in the praise of God and, therefore, in all of life. Faith also gives us strength and motivation to bear each other's burdens.

I was deeply saddened once when I heard a priest boasting that he never had any faith-experience, while looking condescendingly on priests and lay people who spoke about sharing faith-experience. Poor man! What the world needs is not Christians who have memorized knowledge about the truths and duties of faith. What both church and world need most are believers who are seized by faith-experience and have the great privilege of living with Christians who are on fire, filled with the joy and marvel of their faith. Where such communities exist there is credible witness to the gospel and a consciousness of being sent to share the joy of peace and the gospel of peace.

The gospel was and is spread by Christians who are deeply touched by its truths, touched by the unlimited love of God revealed and made tangible in Jesus Christ, and revealed again and again in the lives of saints who direct all our attention to Christ and the Father.

Saints are not looking for a thousand small pleasures, not constantly concerned about their 'self-fulfilment'. They are willing to bear their own cross and the burden of each other. The secret of this was already expressed by the priest Ezra of the Old Testament: "Joy in the Lord is your strength" (Neh 8 : 10).

Mature Christians look at the moral implications of faith with the same trust as at the divine promises. Deeply impressed and changed by his encounter with St Francis of Assisi, a Roman cardinal described the life and message of the saint as being: "We can, we will, we must live the gospel." The 'must' is plain joy, gratitude and strength arising by grace from the 'we can'. This is part of the inner dynamics of love. It makes the saints witnesses and a challenge for many people. They are, themselves, attractive invitations to the feast of faith and to a firm commitment to the kingdom of God.

Faith implies the conviction that we are invited to be friends of Jesus, children of his Father. That allows no mediocrity. "This is the will of God, that you should be holy" (1 Thess 4 : 3). Whoever accepts this vocation is a blessing for his neighbours, for it implies also that "there must be no limit to your goodness, as your heavenly Father's goodness knows no bounds" (Mt 5 : 48).

Christian men and women consider their own vocation to fullness of life, love, justice and peace within the calling of the whole church to holiness. They know, therefore, that their fidelity concerns all the members of the mystical body of Christ, indeed, all of humankind. "If one organ suffers, they all suffer together. If one flourishes, they all rejoice together" (1 Cor 12 : 26).

Our faith is marked by our pilgrim condition. The fundamental option implied in our faith-response tends gradually to permeate our whole being, making us more and more conformed with Christ, more detached from whatever might block our pilgrim way, and freer to join God in his liberating love for people. "Then put on the garments that suit God's chosen people, his own, his beloved: compassion, kindness, humility, gentleness, patience. Be forbearing with one another, and forgiving, where any of you has cause for complaint: you must forgive as the Lord forgave you. To crown all, there must be love, to bind all together and complete the whole" (Col 3 : 12–14).

People who, by the strength of their faith put all this into practice, help humanity to overcome the spiritual 'energy crisis' which is infinitely more serious than the physical energy crisis.

Saints live neither on an island nor in a ghetto. In "whatever the conditions, duties, and circumstances of their lives (they) will grow in holiness day by day through these very situations, if they accept all of them with faith from the hand of their heavenly Father, and if they cooperate with the divine will by showing every man through their earthly activities the love with which God has loved the world" (*The Church*, 41).

*　　　*　　　*

God, our Father, we praise you for the gift of faith which, in so many holy people, has borne fruit in love for the life of the world. We thank you for having revealed in your beloved Son, Jesus Christ, your wonderful design for us and for all men and women. We thank you for the community of faith, the church, for all believers who radiate joy and peace and help us to understand what faith really is.

I thank you for my parents who enriched us children and many friends by the strength and fruitfulness of their faith. Through faith they learned to treat us as sharers of the eternal heritage. We thank you for the witness of dying believers who have given us glimpses of what faith hopes for and the kind of peace it radiates.

Lord Jesus, you have seen your mission to proclaim good news to the poor, the downtrodden, the suffering. You have awakened in many sick and depressed people a new hope and a faith of which you can say, 'Your faith has healed you'. Grant us a radiant faith, and grant to the world — which is so impoverished despite all its material success — what it needs most: saints, joyful, authentic believers.

CHAPTER EIGHT

The Christian and his unbelieving neighbour

> "Be not perturbed, but hold the Lord Christ in reverence in your hearts. Be always ready with your defence whenever you are called to account for the hope that is in you, but make that defence with modesty and respect. Keep your conscience clear, so that when you are abused, those who malign your conduct may be put to shame" (1 Pet 3 : 13–16).

> "Let us make our approach in sincerity of heart and full assurance of faith, our guilty hearts sprinkled clean, our bodies washed with pure water. Let us be firm and unswerving in the confession of our hope, for the Giver of the promise may be trusted. We ought to see how each of us may best arouse others to love and active goodness, not staying away from our meetings, as some do, but rather encouraging one another, all the more because you see the Day drawing near" (Heb 10 : 22–25).

IN the train the passenger seated next to me unburdened himself. His only son, to whom he had intended to hand over his big enterprise, had lost the faith. All the money which the father gave to his son seemed to burn in his hands; he promptly gave it to the poor, arguing that his father's whole wealth was the result of an unjust system. Yet the son became angry when his father gave funds to pious or charitable works, saying that this, as well as his father's faith, was escapism, the unconscious hypocrisy of rich men who treat their workers and employees as objects . . .

We had a long dialogue, and the man made a heart-searching examination of conscience. It was quite clear that his son's loss of faith was of much greater concern to him than the future of his enterprise. He was willing to change his conduct radically in the economic and political spheres, with no other intention than finally to give his son and others a convincing witness of faith.

I had a similar experience when I lectured in the Philippines on the social implications of the sermon on the mount. A very wealthy lady, the owner of large sugar plantations, got a healthy shock. She realized that the conduct of landlords like her was causing a deep crisis of faith in their workers, who lived in misery and were totally dependent. She came to me with the cry, 'Help us!' She was willing to make the most radical changes, giving all who worked on her grounds a full share in the decision processes and fruits of the work. But she felt threatened by the powerful landlord class which would treat her as a traitor if she dared to act according to her conscience. But I did hear her and some other landlords saying, "We must change if we don't want to be accountable for the crises of faith and the rebellion of many!"

One of the most alarming and challenging signs of our times is that almost all of us have some unbelieving relatives, friends or neighbours, and we cannot avoid the hard question whether we might have some accountability for this situation.

The number of 'unchurched' people is rapidly growing in many countries of the western world. Our culture is marked to a considerable extent by a tendency towards unbelief, with little room left for God in the ordering of our social, cultural and economic world. And a large part of the earth is dominated by a party bureaucracy that uses all its power, from education to secret police, from legislation to systematic manipulation of citizens' minds by the mass media, to inculcate its atheism in the dominated people.

But this is not the only form of today's atheism. If it were, atheistic communism would not have much chance to survive, because of its bitter fruits. If the rest of the world were composed of authentic believers, who bear fruit in love and justice for the life of the world, atheistic marxism would be easily unmasked in its naked misery. One has to be blind not to see the bitter fruits. But the question arises: "To what extent are most of us at least partially blind?"

The Second Vatican Council, with sincere heart-searching, concerned itself with the problem of today's atheism (*On The Church in the Modern World*, 19–22) and all christian men and women should meditate on this text and make their personal examination of conscience.

The Council faces the problem with the same earnestness and from approximately the same angle as the wealthy father of the unbelieving son with whom we opened this chapter. The church leaders asked themselves — also in our name — to what extent are we accountable for the increasing unbelief in the world. The shocking phenomenon of atheism in our near neighbourhoods urges us even to ask ourselves about the 'hidden atheist' in our own heart, mind and conduct. We should, however, avoid extremism even in this humble quest. We should not impute to ourselves and the church institutions such guilt as would seem to leave the atheist guiltless.

Our first wholesome reaction is to draw closer in the community of faith, to strengthen and deepen our faith and the faith of our believing brothers and sisters. Then, in a shared effort, we can more easily rid ourselves of any contamination of atheism and expel it from its hiding places in our heart and life-style. Our main concern, in view of the mission of the church and the needs of the world, should be to give a convincing witness of our faith and final hope.

The Council's reflections and analysis about the various forms and shades of atheism are to be understood as an eye-opener and a ringing call to a more radical conversion to faith and all its implications in life. For this purpose I want to draw attention to the main problems.

Today's achiever-consumer society offers an educational system totally geared to raising successful functionaries, business and professional people and scientists, but which gives little attention to the formation of mature personalities with depth and breadth of vision and firmness of character.

Critical youth point to the 'specialist borné, the one-track specialist. The educational system and the whole success-oriented life-style seduce young people and adults to cultivate, intensively and almost exclusively, knowledge for dominion, utility, success and career, with no room left for knowledge of wholeness and salvation. Even the behavioural sciences, which otherwise could make a valuable contribution for human growth, frequently deprive themselves of their beneficial dynamics by concentrating on a small sector of research. Thus the spirit of wholeness is lost.

If we are truly concerned about our unbelieving brothers and sisters, and especially our youth, then we shall do all we can to change for the better our educational system and life-style. If we ourselves, by the grace of God, possess a sense for the Mystery and a vision of wholeness, then we shall support every effort to make this sense and this vision possible in our culture. If all of us strive for wholeness and holiness ourselves, then we can more easily hope that God will grant in our time many saints who are outstanding in these precious qualities.

Ernst Bloch, the marxist philosopher of hope, embodies in his writings one characteristic dimension of the atheist: he cannot and will not believe in a God above us because he refuses to be anybody's debtor. He thinks that it undermines man's dignity to thank a God for having granted us unmerited gifts. Could not our life and behaviour as believers make it more evident that it is this very gratitude and the consciousness that everything is a gift of God that awaken our creativity and foster respect and care for others?

There are unbelievers who want to postpone or eliminate the God question in order to honour man more effectively as supreme purpose, purpose in himself. Could not, should not believers show more convincingly that faith discovers the full dignity of every human being, and that nothing can move them more to respect the dignity and liberty of all people than our faith that God has created them in his image and likeness?

The Council alerts us to the fact that there are 'unbelievers' who in reality do not deny the true God but are protesting against a man-made, false image of God. Could not we believers, through a more fervent hunger and thirst for a better knowledge of the true God, and through adoration 'in spirit and truth', help these people to discover explicitly their own yearning for the true God? What this demands of us, above all, is to see in Jesus Christ the true image of the Father who reveals himself in Christ, and to be most vigilant against every temptation to make ourselves a self-styled 'image of God'.

The most dangerous and perhaps the most common form of *Godlessness* (I choose the expression consciously) is the absolute lack of interest in the God question, coupled with the same lack of interest in an ultimate sense of life. Some modern godless people are not even interested enough to deny God's existence or to think or speak about these questions. Their interest is totally oriented to success, power, pleasure and similiar things.

This form of godlessness is the strongest challenge for us Christians. We surely cannot heal this estrangement if the same transient and disintegrated interests occupy the first place in our own thinking and life-style, even though we also — but in second place — are seeking to know God and serve him. This widespread *also* is, in itself, an expression of polytheism: we have other gods side by side with the true God if we do not reserve for God the first place, indeed, the whole place in our hearts.

The biblical texts at the beginning of this chapter show us that words alone are not convincing and liberating answers to the problems, wounds and needs of our unbelieving neighbour. Intelligence and competence in dialogue are surely not to be depreciated, but the first condition is total witness by our life. Then the words and gestures will arise from a joyous, grateful faith and a profound trust in the divine promises.

Faith and life must be harmonized, but never in the direction of the lowest or mediocre denominator. If there is a painful distance between the loftiness of our faith and the quasi-mediocrity of our life, our unbelieving neighbour should be able to least to sense how much this pains us and how sincerely we are striving to overcome the gap.

Our reflections on our unbelieving relatives should not be confused with the painful experience of good christian parents when their children go through a crisis of faith and, in some cases, tell their parents that they have lost their faith. This is a very complex phenomenon, differing from case to case, but often sharpened by the impact of an atheistic or secularist environment in school, in the mass media and in the general environment.

I can exemplify this parental experience and this struggle of youth during such crises. Fervent parents asked me to arrange an appointment for one of their daughters. The girl came willingly and spoke with true sincerity. She had told her parents that she could no longer receive the sacraments because she had lost her faith. At a certain point in our dialogue I asked her if this quest was her greatest concern. She said simply, 'Yes'; but she qualified it later by saying, 'Maybe my greatest concern is the fear that I shall not be able to give to the children, whom I hope to have, the joyous faith that has marked my parents' life."

I told her clearly: "As I see it, you are by no means an unbeliever. As long as this quest takes the first place in your heart and mind, God will accept it as though you could believe without any trouble. Perhaps you are now closer to God than you were in your uncritical phase." Indeed, she was on the road to a more mature faith. Can all those who consider themselves believers and pious Christians sincerely say that the concern to know God and to do his will takes first place in their life?

Another experience touched my heart deeply. A zealous family had three healthy children and an almost-blind son. The members of the family were always cheerful with the blind boy but they never dared to talk directly about his blindness. For a considerable time everything went well. The boy received first communion with great fervour, and for two years he received the sacrament each Sunday with his parents and his brothers. But one Sunday he did not join them when they went to communion. The parents thought it best not to question this; but when the day came on which it was his turn to say the blessing at table, he said firmly: "I don't pray any more; I cannot believe that God is good."

For some years this situation continued. No change seemed to be under way until he began to speak with his parents about his handicap and all its consequences. He declared explicitly his doubt about God's goodness and justice, but his words now were more like a question and a quest. Gradually the family felt that he had begun to accept his handicap. Then one Sunday he went with the parents to communion, and this time he gave the explanation immediately. "I can believe and pray again." A little later he said: "I think I am now mature enough to receive confirmation. I know now what it means to be a Christian."

In both cases the children were blessed with parents who gave them the support of trust, abiding love and respect, and left them time to find their way through the crisis. In both cases also, I could clearly see a growth of faith in the whole family.

* * *

Gracious Father, I thank you for the gift of faith. It is due to your grace and patience that, in spite of the lag between my faith and my life, no rupture happened; and under the favourable impact of so many wonderful believers my faith could grow and become more deeply rooted. Praised be your graciousness forever!

Help us to understand our unbelieving or seemingly unbelieving neighbour. Let us, when possible, tell him or her the right word at the right time, and let us accept the challenge of this situation by making a firmer decision to live according to our faith, deepening it in all its dimensions.

Holy God, send forth your Spirit, that we Christians, all together, may find ways to heal our culture which becomes for so many a cause of unbelief. Inspire us to form a more lively community of believers and to seek light and strength from the celebration of the sacraments of faith. Help us to take our mission to be 'light for the world' more seriously.

Father of us all, assist parents who are at a loss when facing the dire crisis of faith in their children. Guide young people in the dark days of crises so that they may find their way to a mature and firm faith.

CHAPTER NINE

Creative fidelity

"Here are words you may trust:
If we died with him, we shall live with him;
If we endure, we shall reign with him.
If we deny him, he will deny us.
If we are faithless, he keeps faith,
for he cannot deny himself" (2 Tim 2:11–13).

"I am always thanking God for you. I thank him for his grace given to you in Christ Jesus. I thank him for the enrichment that has come to you in Christ. You possess full knowledge and you can give expression to it, because in you the evidence for the truth of Christ has found confirmation. There is indeed no single gift you lack, while you wait expectantly for our Lord Jesus Christ to reveal himself. He will keep you firm to the end, without reproach on the Day of our Lord Jesus. It is God himself who called you to share in the life of his Son Jesus Christ our Lord; and God keeps faith" (1 Cor 1:4–9).

NEXT to atheism, one of the most alarming signs of our times is the shocking lack of faithfulness. What good are Christians for the salvation of the world if, through adultery and even divorce, they break the covenant of marriage in almost the same proportions as unbelievers? A lack of faithfulness is a sign of lack of faith. Where there is unselfish faithfulness and generous forgiveness, there is proximity of faith. The world needs both the joyous faith and the unbroken faithfulness of the saints.

Holy scripture sings in many melodies the praise of faithfulness — however, of human fidelity only in view of God's own faithfulness to covenant and promises. We praise God, above all, for his saving justice and mercy by which he restores faithless sinners to renewed constancy. God himself praises the faithful servant and steward in whom he finds a mirror-image of his own faithfulness which invites all of us to this stalwart virtue.

Our fundamental option of faith is at the same time a vow of fidelity. If in faith we entrust ourselves totally to God, we will praise him through our constancy. The more firmly we walk on the road of faithfulness, the more our faith comes to its full development.

In the sacraments of faith the believer consciously meets God's favour and faithfulness. In fruitful celebration we affirm our grateful acceptance of our vocation in allegiance to the covenant by which God binds himself to his people and calls them to mutual fidelity. Our whole christian life should echo the 'Amen' of the liturgy in which we solemnly say our 'Yes' to him who, by his faithfulness, calls us to abiding fidelity.

St Paul explains the deep meaning of the liturgical 'Amen' in view of God's enduring trustworthiness. "As God is true, the language in which we address you is not an ambiguous blend of Yes and No. The Son of God, Christ Jesus, proclaimed among you by us . . . was never a blend of Yes and No. With him it was, and is, Yes. He is the Yes pronounced upon God's promises, every one of them. That is why, when we give glory to God, it is through Christ Jesus that we say 'Amen'. And if you and we belong to Christ, guaranteed as his and anointed, it is all God's doing; it is God also who has set his seal upon us, and as a pledge of what is to come has given the Spirit to dwell in our hearts" (2 Cor 1:18–22). Whenever we say 'Amen' in our prayers, it should be a conscious, trustful confirmation of our fundamental option for faith and fidelity, to the praise of God's own faithfulness.

Jesus is the supreme sign and sacrament of God's faithfulness in his covenant with humankind. In Jesus Christ and by the power of his Spirit he restores us in the covenant and calls us to a renewed and growing fidelity. Christ is the abiding sign of both God's efficacious grace and humanity's response, since, having come from the Father, he has given once and forever his faithful response to the Father in the name of redeemed humanity.

Jesus' faithfulness to the Father's design and covenant proves itself in his total readiness for solidarity with us sinful human beings. He who has taken upon himself the burden of our sins and our misery thereby calls us by the gifts of the Spirit to bear each other's burdens. Faithfulness to his fidelity makes his disciples one with each other and light for the world (cf. Jn 17: 11–21).

If we hope to conform ourselves to Christ's faithfulness and become effective signs of his call to fidelity to the world, we have to rid ourselves of wrong ideas about what faithfulness is. A static and stagnant society and one's yearning to remain in such a culture when it has gone, have seduced many to confuse fidelity with habit, passivity, hang-ups or a clinging to human traditions which either have lost their original meaning or have never been signs of faithfulness of God's holy presence.

Lessons from the prophets and saints give us courage to live the gospel and faithfully proclaim it ever anew, in consciousness of God's nearness to his pilgrim people, even when this means leaving the beaten paths on which many still tread. St Francis of Assisi was one of many saints who were first considered to be fools or dangerous innovators.

Faithfulness that arises from a living faith has nothing to do with blind submissiveness or unspirited observance of external laws. Christians who are guided by the Spirit know the ultimate law of faithful love and the deepest meaning of all authentic laws. Their loyalties to causes and groups will always be measured by fidelity to Christ. By faithfully following in his footsteps they can unmask any undeserved loyalties.

The 'Yes' to God's calling to faithfulness implies the courage to take risks, to set out on new roads when necessary, as Abraham, the prophets, the saints, and especially Jesus did in the history of salvation. Faithfulness to the gospel guarantees christian identity, but it does so by calling us to a continuing process of conversion and growth, to an ever more creative and generous fidelity.

Our faithfulness to the church is much more than mere observance of her laws. For her mission and her inner growth the church needs Christians who make creative use of their charisms and competences. The faithful servant does not bury his talent in the earth so that it can be given back without risk (cf. Mt 25: 21). What christian faithfulness means is best expressed by the biblical message of the gifts and fruits of the Spirit. Fidelity to the Spirit is creativity for the life of the world.

Those guided by the Spirit know that true faithfulness to one's own identity and vocation is possible only in faithfulness to

God and in solidarity with the children of God. We find our true self in loving service to God and fellowmen.

Fidelity to oneself must be realistic even in the case of devout believers. Our 'I-believe' is still mixed with a partial and sometimes hidden 'I-do-not-yet-wholly-believe.' That means: 'I need a further conversion to greater coherence with faith and with my fundamental option to faithfulness.' The more we praise God for his faithfulness the more truthful will be our 'I-believe'.

In our response to God's fidelity we can discover the grace-filled possibilities of fidelity among men. Faithfulness to God is the solid foundation of all human constancy. This, in turn, is an indispensable experience and expression of our response to God's undeserved fidelity to us poor sinners. But among humans, constancy has its limits in our 'Amen' to God. It is authentic only if we are on the road together to an ever more thorough fidelity to God.

The covenant of fidelity between two persons in marriage is a risk, since both partners are sources of risk. The same is somehow true of religious vows where the consecration to God's reign implies a covenant between the community and the individual. Yet we can dare this risk without anguish if our mutual 'Yes' is given and integrated into the covenant with God, the source of all human fidelity. Time and again we are forced to submit ourselves humbly to God's healing and forgiving faithfulness. There we also learn mutual reconciliation and forgiveness as an essential part of covenant fidelity.

Even if a marriage covenant is broken by one of the partners to the point that healing has become impossible, although the other partner has done all in his or her power to save the covenant, the faithfulness of forgiving love must report its victory in the heart of the abandoned spouse. A refusal to forgive the pain caused by the other's infidelity can destroy the integrity and health of the 'innocent' person. In the eyes of God, indeed, nobody is 'innocent' if he or she does not forgive in conformity with God's merciful and healing fidelity.

In holy scripture God admonishes us in many ways to be faithful unto death. The divine warnings given to the unfaithful servant are to be seen in the context of God's promises that he wills to perfect the work that he has begun. On his part, nothing will be lacking if we turn to him in humble and faithful prayer.

There is no doubt about the teaching of the church that the grace of perseverance unto death is an undeserved gift. It is equally undoubtable, moreover, that God wants to give this grace to all the redeemed. We pray sincerely for this gift while constantly striving to honour God's saving faithfulness by forgiving and healing faithfulness towards our fellow travellers. My feeling is that not enough is preached and written today on this essential dimension of christian life.

The prayer and effort for final perseverance are not at all a withdrawal into anguished care for one's own self. On the contrary, the legitimate interest in one's salvation implies total dedication to God's reign and the kingdom of love, justice and peace. We do not forget for a moment that salvation and holiness imply solidarity; but only a fool would imagine the possibility of being helpful to the salvation, well-being and faithfulness of the world while neglecting his own salvation and faithfulness to God's gracious love.

*   *   *

We praise you, Father! Faithful to your name and in unlimited mercy, you have not abandoned sinful humankind in its self-caused misery. In your faithfulness you have gone so far as to send us your only-begotten Son as the faithful sign and witness of your holiness, love and mercy.

We praise your glory, for in the history of creation and salvation you have chosen us to be not only recipients but also coworkers and witnesses of your faithfulness and mercy, and have not divested us of this wonderful dignity in spite of our failures.

We thank you, Lord Jesus Christ, that in the work of redemption you have sealed the Father's and your own faithfulness with the blood of the covenant on the cross. We thank you for having offered to the Father, in the name of all humankind whom you came to redeem, your most precious tribute of faithfulness and have called us to join you in praise of the Father by a life renewed in fidelity.

Lord Jesus, send us from the Father the Holy Spirit to teach us how to be free for your kingdom and to be faithful servants and witnesses for the life of the world which is so much in need of fidelity.

CHAPTER TEN

Gracious and faithful encounter with the aged

"Despise no man for being old;
some of us are growing old as well. . . .
Do not ignore the discourse of your elders,
for they themselves learned from their fathers;
they can teach you to understand
and to have an answer ready in time of need"

(Ecclus 8 : 6–9).

"If you have not gathered wisdom in your youth,
how will you find it when you are old?
Sound judgement sits well on grey hairs
and wise advice comes well from older men.
Wisdom is fitting in the aged,
and ripe counsel in men of eminence.
Long experience is the old man's crown,
and his pride is the fear of the Lord" (Ecclus 25 : 3–6).

A new branch of science has developed during the last decades: gerontology, knowledge about ageing and the aged, their social role and their somatic, psychic and social problems. Our relationship to the aged and what their social relevance is reveal our fidelity to the past or our lack of it. In the western world the social problem of the aged is acute and, in many aspects, a symptom of a sick society.

In every age there has been a generation problem. In the holy scriptures we find many words of wisdom about attitudes towards the old, and there evidently was a need to urge the younger generations to honour the aged and to learn from their knowledge. But there is ample evidence also that generally the culture of the biblical era showed great reverence and a sense of gratitude towards the aged.

In our times the generation problem has become acute. In a time of rapid cultural change the dialogue between the genera-

E

tions has tremendous importance, but it also becomes much more difficult. The cultural diversity between the new and older generation — present even in the vocabulary — has heightened the barriers to mutual understanding and enrichment. The horizon of understanding has changed deeply and so has the distance between old and young. The latest statistic of the Federal Republic of Germany, for instance, tells us that only 8% of the people over 65 years of age live in a household with children or grandchildren.

Not infrequently the elderly have the feeling of being side-tracked. This feeling is particularly strong in nursing homes which are run according to economic considerations alone. In most of the industrialized and urban countries the suicide rate among the old is very high. Often it is preceded by the painful feeling of a kind of social death, a saddening experience of being considered 'useless'. In the mass media and even in parliaments there is discussion of the 'right' of the old and sick to euthanasia. The elderly who feel put aside understand this talk as an indirect invitation to disappear from the theatre of life. This, of course, is not just a problem for the aged; it is a shocking indication of a sick society.

Two generations ago it was a serious social problem in rural areas when the old did not hand over their farm or enterprise to the younger generation at the proper time. Today men and women retire from their professional activities when they reach 60 or 65, often when they are still vigorous and not at all ready to become inactive. Many are unprepared for the sudden change and do not know how to profit by their leisure time or to find an activity that interests them. This is especially true of those who have no meaningful social and cultural contacts, no real friendships.

Add to this the high inflation rate in many countries whereby the state robs them of their savings. And even where a high standard of social security prevails, bureaucratic 'slopwork' causes distress in some cases. Single women are still widely discriminated against. What women have done in household and education is not honoured as socially important work, and even for paid jobs they do not receive pay or pensions equal to men's.

While in earlier times senior citizens could be proud of their role and their dignity as elders, the modern cult of youthfulness deprives them of this satisfaction. All this aggravates the task of ageing: of accepting the many ailments, the gradual loss of hearing, the diminution of sight and strength.

Yet not all the picture is dark. Much has been done and is being done in many countries to ease the end of life's journey for the elderly. However, the longer life-span and the consequent increased proportion of elderly citizens forces all of us — church, state, families, trade unions, individuals — to give serious thought to how best to approach the social problems of the aged.

In the church of the first centuries the aged were community leaders or at least advisers. The term 'elders' (presbiteri) for priests arose from this situation. It shows that the older people, the elders, were active in the apostolate. Today in some countries the church recruits many vocations for the permanent diaconate and even for the priesthood from the ranks of the 'retired': those still vigorous and willing to use their energies and life-experience in the service of God's kingdom and their neighbours.

A considerable number of senior citizens show a hunger for ongoing education. Church and society should make this and other appropriate privileges and outlets available for them so that their knowledge and life-experience may be fruitful for themselves and for others.

One of the saddest aspects of the aged is loneliness. Let us remember that to visit the sick and the lonely is an important 'work of mercy'. But this must not be a condescending mercy which might offend the lonely. If we visit the aged, we want to let them feel that we enjoy listening to them and learning from them. Especially their children and grandchildren should feel privileged if they have good contact with parents and grandparents.

The aged, who feel lonely but are still spiritually and physically strong, could best overcome their loneliness by visiting other ailing and lonely people, by offering them some services, reading to them, helping them to pray. In this context we understand better the well-known text of James' epistle: "Is one of you ill? He should send for the elders of the congregation to pray over him and anoint him with oil in the name of the Lord" (5 : 14).

From the 'houses of prayer' in the United States and other

countries came valuable inspirations and initiatives in this sense. Not only the younger members of houses of prayer but especially the senior sisters, who had learned spontaneous shared prayer and the dialogue of faith, dedicated themselves most vigorously to the lonely and sick, bringing them consolation and deeper understanding of their situation.

Many nuns, who had behind them successful careers in teaching, found this apostolate the highlight of their life. Bishops allowed them to bring holy communion to the lonely and sick. Some of these aged people who had found great consolation from the visiting nuns or lay people wrote to their bishops asking why these holy women were not allowed to administer the sacrament of the anointing of the sick. They reasoned: "The priest is always in a hurry, rushing in for the rite and rushing out, while the nuns take time to listen to us and help us to grasp the meaning of sickness and suffering." At the present time theological insights do not allow this special ministry to people not ordained. But senior citizens can visit the lonely and console them with the dialogue of faith and prayers. And, in a way, that has much to do with the 'anointing' of which the letter of James speaks.

In this matter much more could be done. But the priority we give to this spiritual and pastoral dimension does not at all dispense us from shared efforts to face the social problems of the aged in our culture.

*   *   *

Lord, we thank you for the gift of our older brothers and sisters, for their wisdom, kindness, life experience and their willingness to share them with us. We thank you especially for those old men and women who radiate holiness and joy. Grant that we and our youth may gladly follow the guidance which you give through holy scripture for our encounter with the aged.

Assist the old and lonely who are hurt by neglect and social estrangement. Help them to resolve their problems and find meaning for their sufferings in the spirit of faith. Illumine them on how to make creative use of their years and days which you are adding for their final growth and the benefit of others.

Lord, inspire the influential men and women in state and

society to resolve the sometimes shocking problems of the aged and to overcome all kinds of injustice under which they suffer today.

Guide your church so that, following the first generations of her existence, she may be vigilant, wise and courageous in giving the aged, who are willing and able, the best opportunities to bring all their capacities and their generosity home to her apostolate.

CHAPTER ELEVEN

Let youth have a chance

"I write to you, fathers, because you know him who is and has been from the beginning.
I write to you, young men, because you have mastered the evil one.
To you, children, I have written because you know the Father.
To you, fathers, I have written because you know him who is and has been from the beginning.
To you, young men, I have written because you are strong; God's word remains in you, and you have mastered the evil one" (1 Jn 2:13–14).

"Never be harsh with an elder; appeal to him as if he were your father. Treat the younger men as brothers, the older women as mothers, and the younger as your sisters, in all purity" (1 Tim 5:1–2).

IF the aged are an invitation to gratitude and faithfulness to the past, the young are a challenge to hope and a commitment to the future. Of course, all our relationships must be marked by grateful appreciation as we remember the past, by vigilance for the opportunities of the here and now, and by hope opening to the absolute future.

Our hope, which looks to the promises of salvation history, and our responsibility for our own future and the future of humankind will determine our attitude towards youth. A decisive question for the future of society and church is our investment in caring for youth, in educating our children and adolescents for coresponsibility. An open-minded dialogue with youth will keep us spiritually young.

In this perspective we can see more clearly the problems raised by responsible parenthood: the conscious decisions of responsibility in the transmission of life and in education. This is the most valuable investment for humanity's future if the transmission of life and a good life-style are accompanied by the transmission of faith, hope and love.

Many married couples refuse to transmit life because they have no gratitude for the past, no trust in the future, and no discovery of the preciousness of the present moment. Others are simply discouraged by the difficulty of educating children properly in our disordered society. But couples who are blessed by mutual love, filled with gratitude for the gift of life and the hope of life everlasting, and able to make the most creative use of the present opportunities, will always have the courage to say 'Yes' to their parental vocation.

Responsible parenthood implies today, much more than in an earlier, more static society, an education totally geared to the formation of responsible men and women. In a uniformed, harmonious culture a common faithfulness to inherited traditions and customs served to integrate the children into the given culture and its values. In this frame the respect which the first letter to Timothy (above) speaks about was quite possible: parents treating their children like brothers and sisters in Christ, as coheirs of eternal life. In that closed society a 'good education' meant also a genuine interiorization of faith, hope and love, and of everything that is good, true and beautiful.

For christian parents the goals of education are essentially the same today; but the newness of the situation requires a different emphasis and some additional perspectives.

The new horizon is determined by a rapid cultural change, a pluralism of world views and life-styles, a tremendous influence of the mass media. For many children TV is the new foster mother. Hence, an emphasis on adaptation to the given influences — especially if coupled with a training or personal tendency to blind obedience — would be simply a catastrophe. A prevalent passivity and submissiveness in childhood could lead either to rebellion during adolescence and/or to submissiveness to the prevalent forces of the environment into which the young adult will be thrown.

The main emphasis in education, therefore, must be on becoming responsible and discerning persons. The old values are not disowned but should be subordinated and integrated into a vision of wholeness, holiness, responsibility and discernment.

Outside the christian family our young people hear much talk about freedom, protest and personal identity in self-fulfilment, but little about faithfulness to God and fellowmen and about self-critique. It is especially important, therefore, that christian education should explain and cultivate, by witness and word, freedom in Christ, respect for the freedom and conscience of others, identity in healthy relationships with God and fellowmen, creative faithfulness and discernment which includes healthy self-examination.

Parents, members of the family, teachers and pastors must be aware that it is normal for youth to go through certain crises — for instance, through a phase of protest and sharp questioning. Without profiting from this phase there might be little hope that the adolescents and young adults would be able to withstand the many dangers of being manipulated by ideologies or by the pressure of prevalent trends working especially through the various mass media.

Adults and ageing people have to learn, again and again anew, how to dialogue with young people since their reactions change considerably within a few years. We have also to free ourselves from a stereotyped idea about youth. There is an enormous diversity of groups, and within the group each adolescent has a right to be seen in his or her uniqueness.

The phase of entrance into adulthood requires maturation for the great decisions of life: in the first place a consolidated option for faithfulness to God and his kingdom, the choice of a state of life, of vocation, and eventually the choice of mate. Youth should be encouraged by the adult to learn that a clear identity depends on a firm bond of faithfulness. From the firmness and coherence of our own character, children and adolescents should see how the great decisions of life are built on a faithfulness to conscience even in minor matters.

Young Christians should learn also to see how life's decisions, great or small, made in fidelity to one's fundamental option, gain light, firmness and beauty in the light of the sacraments: how the baptismal vow is confirmed and deepened by the vow of confirmation, purified and strengthened by the gifts and fruits of the Holy Spirit (cf. Gal 5:22). These are the weapons for fighting against man's incarnate selfishness — in which collective and individual selfishness are frequently allies.

Participation by youth in church or civic groups and associations should help them to develop and to exercise their creative energies. Adolescents and young adults should be treated as partners and given credit in coresponsibility.

The extended period of learning in our educational systems brings some danger that youth may swallow the huge educational material only passively. All those responsible for education in family, school, society and state should give young people enough chance and challenge for cooperation in creative liberty and fidelity.

This should occur also in political circles. A party in which the old men are clinging to their chairs punishes itself and jeopardizes its future. There is surely a treasure of experience and wisdom in those who have grown up in dignity and have competently taken their share of responsibility; but if one thinks himself to be irreplaceable, this is not a sign of wisdom. Green light for ability implies also green light for youth willing to acquire competence and able to share in responsibility. In all sectors of public life, in society and church, we need the élan, courage and imagination of youth.

Throughout the world the unemployment of youth is a most serious and frightening problem. Not without urgent reasons does Pope John Paul II constantly insist that the effective dealing with this phenomenon should have high priority. Long-lasting unemployment is not only a grave danger for the psychic and social life of youth but also a great loss for society. It should be evident to all those responsible that it is easier to create jobs for youth than to free youth from drug-addiction, alcoholism and violence once they become slaves of these evils.

A distinctively christian vision of hope and solidarity gives us strong motivation to help children and youth to discover and to cultivate the contemplative dimensions of life, to learn to find in prayer the synthesis and integration of life. A considerable part of today's youth is open for the dialogue of faith, for shared prayer, for joy in the praise of God — provided, however, that there is no suspicion of formalism. They are in search of authentic religious experience . . . They need saints.

*   *   *

God, our Father, Lord of history, you love children and youth. You rejoice in their growth towards maturity. You can give to us adults and ageing people youthful opennness and joy in creative activities. Look down with favour upon youth for whom today's culture can be a great challenge but also, alas, a great danger.

Grant young men and women the courage to be faithful, to accept their share of responsibility, and an ardent yearning to discover life's ultimate meaning and purpose, trust in you and a reasonable trust in the future of humanity which depends so much on their active participation in shaping it.

Give to us adults and senior citizens the art and the willingness to accept youth, to love them as they are, and also because they are different from us and can offer dimensions which we are no longer able to offer. Help us to accept them fully as fellow travellers and partners on the road to eternal life and, in the effort, to shape future history to the benefit of coming generations. Give us finally also the courage to learn from youth.

Grant to your church the prophetic vision and freedom to rid herself of dead and deadly traditions and ossifications, so that she can proclaim the gospel to you and live it in its abiding freshness and newness, thus to meet the ready generosity of youth to be active members in the work for your kingdom.

CHAPTER TWELVE

Glorify God in your body

" 'Destroy this temple,' Jesus replied, 'and in three days I will raise it again.' They said, 'It has taken forty-six years to build this temple. Are you going to raise it again in three days?' But the temple he was speaking of was his body. After his resurrection his disciples recalled what he had said, and they believed the Scripture and the words that Jesus had spoken" (Jn 2 : 19–22).

"Wherever we go we carry death with us in our body, the death that Jesus died, that in this body also life may reveal itself, the life that Jesus lives. For continually, while still alive, we are being surrendered into the hands of death, for Jesus' sake, so that the life of Jesus also may be revealed in this mortal body of ours. Thus death is at work in us, and life in you. But Scripture says, 'I believed, and therefore I spoke out', and we too, in the same spirit of faith, believe and therefore speak out; for we know that he who raised the Lord Jesus to life will with Jesus raise us too, and bring us to his presence, and you with us" (2 Cor 4 : 10–14).

THE whole human person in all its bodily and spiritual reality should be and become more and more an attractive image of God. A human countenance radiating joy, peace, kindness, gentleness, cordiality, compassion can awaken in others a great longing to see God's glorious countenance in Jesus Christ. The hands of faithful people resting in each other's, guaranteeing trust and understanding, can make it easier for many to pray to God, 'Into thy hands I commit my spirit.' We stretch out our hands as a sign of cordial greeting or of reconciliation and accept gratefully the other's hand as a sign of friendship and fidelity.

Compared with this basic human experience, we realize how impoverished is the image of man constructed by the master of manipulation, B. R. Skinner, who sees in human hands only the hands of the ape seizing prey or the hands of controllers and controlled masses clapping applause to dictators.

The human body is the basic symbol for discernment of spirits. Do we not know from afar, from the lift of the runner's head and the speed of his feet, that he is a messenger of joy bringing good news? And conversely, when we see the goose-step of men trained for war and oppression, do we not also hear in the distance the noises of war and the cries of the oppressed?

Holy scripture gives us a magnificent vision of the human body. Jesus praises the Father: "Thou hast prepared a body for me . . . Here I am, O God, to do thy will" (Heb 10:5–7). His hands dispense blessing, touch the blind, the deaf, the sick, the lepers with healing love and power. His gracious countenance consoles the afflicted. And finally, on the cross he stretches out his arms in all-embracing love for the whole of humanity. His voice not only echoes the cry of suffering and outcast people but also speaks words of concern, forgiveness, love, consolation and promise. His pierced heart becomes the fountain of salvation.

Jesus himself calls his body a temple in which God is glorified and which, raised to life again by the Father, will be glorious in all eternity. For Christians, therefore, all temples built by human hands take second place to the bodies of the children of God conformed to the body of the beloved Son, Jesus Christ. Christ has given the greatest sign of love by giving up his body on the cross for his brothers and sisters (cf. 1 Jn 3:16). The love of his disciples, too, must be embodied — revealed in their body.

Day by day Jesus offers us the totally-embodied sign of his love with the words: "Take and eat; this is my body; this is the cup of my blood, drink from it."

The Christian's body, consecrated in baptism and sealed by the Spirit in confirmation, must be honoured above all temples on earth, for it is in a unique sense a temple of God, temple of the Holy Spirit (cf. 1 Cor 3:16–17; 6:19; 2 Cor 6:20). Thus the admonition of the apostle, "then honour God in your body" (1 Cor 6:20) becomes a motif of christian life. Our vocation to holiness, a life to the glory of God, is carved into our body. This temple of God, consecrated by God, must be kept holy.

In this same light the christian concept of chastity must be understood. It excludes any kind of contempt for the body and for the sexual dimension of the human person. The motive for chastity is absolutely positive: reverence for our body, for the physical and psychic dimensions of sexuality, reverence for the work of the Creator and Redeemer.

The Christian's prayer is embodied too. We turn our eyes and stretch our arms to heaven as a symbol of turning heart and mind to God. We meditate with all our senses, and the whole visible creation invites us to praise God. Just as it was for King David, so also is it natural for our African Christians to express their joy before the Lord, their trust in God and their surrender to him in sacred dance.

The fundamental truth that the human body, redeemed and consecrated, is a temple concerns more than our prayer. It is a temple which in all times, all circumstances and all activities, in joy and suffering, is destined to the glory of God and the building up of the mystical body of Christ. The first requirement is that the whole person, in and through the body, radiates purity, reverence, peace, trust, fidelity. We are called to be light to the world and salt to the earth in our embodiment. "The lamp of your body is the eye. When your eyes are sound, you have light for your whole body; but when the eyes are bad, you are in darkness. See to it then that the light you have is not darkness. If you have light for your whole body with no trace of darkness, it will all be as bright as when a lamp flashes its rays upon you" (Lk 11: 34–36).

In the light of Christ, man and woman in their bodily realities are a kind of sacrament, an effective sign of hope. The appearance of the human being, made in the image of God and able to cultivate and radiate spiritual values with his body, is a first fulfilment of the divine promises and intentions of creation. It points to a still greater promise, the coming of the Word incarnate, the Word of the Father 'made flesh'. His body on the cross and then glorified is the supreme promise to the whole of creation and already an awesome fulfilment that opens a new future. Jesus, crucified and risen, is the supreme, all-encompassing sacrament of hope for humanity and creation.

He continues to be a visible sign of hope also in his mystical body, the bodily life of his true disciples. They are called to embody this hope through their witness of faith, including their readiness to take upon themselves suffering whenever the victory of love, justice and peace requests it.

This witness to hope implies responsibility to the world, an ecological consciousness that perceptibly attests that Christ is the Saviour of the whole world. "For the created universe waits with eager expectation for God's sons and daughters to be revealed. It was made the victim of frustration, not by its own choice, but because of him who made it so; yet always there was hope, because the universe itself is to be freed from the shackles of mortality and enter upon the liberty and splendour of the children of God. Up to the present, we know, the whole created universe groans in all its parts as if in the pangs of childbirth. Not only so, but even we, to whom the Spirit is given as first-fruits of the harvest to come, are groaning inwardly while we wait for God to . . . set our whole body free" (Rom 8:19–23).

It is God's will that we should train our body and keep it healthy. His design for salvation is for the whole human being. To abuse our body by unhealthy habits or life-style is to sin also against our psychic health and even against our salvation. By living healthily we reach a harmonious wholeness that affords us greater energies not only for work but also for better human relationships and for the art of radiating peace and joy.

But on the other side, our body must never become an idol. This would sharply contradict our mission to 'glorify God in our body'. In a culture in which many people have ceased to be adorers of God, it is hardly surprising that idolatry of the body flourishes. What Paul warns against under other historical circumstances happens all too easily in a luxurious consumer-society: "There are many whose way of life makes them enemies of the cross of Christ. They are heading for destruction, appetite is their god, and they glory in their shame. Their minds are set on earthly things" (Phil 3:18–19). Many overfeed their body to such an extent that their spirit vanishes; their spiritual strength dies. In their idolatrous cult of the body they poison it with nicotine, alcohol, psychotropic drugs and too much food, while millions of people die of starvation.

The sports hero, the year's beauty queen, the movie starlet have become idols and eagerly put themselves on parade as such. They fail to realise that they make a sad show of vanity and spiritual malnutrition. Nothing is to be said against healthy sport, joy in play and dance, decent care for the body's appearance and the admirable art of acting, so long as the scale of values is observed. If we rightly rejoice in the beauty of flowers, why should we not rejoice even more in seeing beautiful men and women whose bodies reveal a beauty tuned into a higher harmony!

*   *   *

Lord, our God, how glorious is your name! What is man that you should remember him, yet you have crowned him with glory and honour (cf. Ps 8:1–7). In his bodily reality he is by no means inferior to angels, since the body of your Son incarnate has glorified you, the Father, and you have revealed in his risen body the fullness of glory and beauty. We thank you for the wonderful work of our body and our calling to honour you in it. We praise you for having revealed that our body is meant to be a temple, sealed and consecrated by the Holy Spirit.

Grant that we may understand this ever better in its implication for our life. Pardon us for having paid so little attention to praising your name in view of our body and that of our neighbour.

Lord Jesus, you have given the Father the greatest honour in your body, even when this was dishonoured on the cross, dishonoured by sinners.

Enlighten us by your Holy Spirit in times of sickness, suffering and in the hour of our death, to adore you and the Father in this, your temple. Grant us joy and admiration for the true beauty of our bodies, as foreshadowing the eternal glory in which they are to shine, and protect us from the danger of making your temple a degraded idol.

CHAPTER THIRTEEN

Chaste language of truth and love

"Then God said, 'Let us make man in our image and likeness to rule the fish in the sea, the birds of heaven, the
cattle, all wild animals on earth' . . . So God created man in
his own image; in the image of God he created him; male
and female he created them. God blessed them and said to
them, 'Be fruitful and increase, fill the earth and subdue
it.' . . .

"Then the Lord God formed a man from the dust of
the ground and breathed into his nostrils the breath of life.
Thus the man became a living creature. . . .

"Then the Lord God said, 'It is not good for the man
to be alone. I will provide a partner for him.' . . . And so
the Lord God put the man into a trance, and while he
slept, he took one of his ribs and closed the flesh over the
place. The Lord God then built up the rib, which he had
taken out of the man, into a woman. He brought her to
the man and the man said:

> 'Now this, at last —
> bone from by bones,
> flesh from my flesh! —
> this shall be called woman,
> for from man was this taken.'

That is why a man leaves his father and mother and is
united to his wife, and the two become one flesh. . . .

"The man called his wife Eve because she was the
mother of all who live" (Gen 1:26–28; 2:7; 2:18–24;
3:20).

ALREADY Genesis sees the origin of man and woman in God
who speaks out his loving design. The gospel brings this into the
full light of God's word: "The Word, then, was with God at
the beginning, and through him all things came to be; no single
thing was created without him" (Jn 1:3).

The whole of creation has somehow the quality of a word, a

revelation. But man and woman in their reciprocity have a special mysterious relationship to God who speaks. 'God said.' The man and the woman come to their own truth and self-knowledge when they discover the depth of language in their mutual complementarity, in being with and for each other, knowing each other in love. With good reason researchers think that the origin of human language is the language of love between man and woman, foreshadowed already in the love songs of the birds and the love calls of other animals.

In biblical imagery woman corresponds to a deep dream, a man's trance; and she too yearns for complementarity and partnership with man. However, this is no empty dream. God himself blesses them when he solemnly speaks, creating them in his own image for communion, companionship in a reciprocity of consciences.

Man and woman should become for each other a truthful 'word', an embodied, life-giving word remindful of the divine covenant of love and a loving Creator. Their 'Yes' to their indissoluble covenant of faithful love and to their vocation to be sharers of God's creative love is crowned by the children, if all help one another to become ever more visibly an image of God.

There is a good biblical basis for today's theological endeavour to treat sexuality as embodied language which, in the marriage covenant and the faithfully-fulfilled parental vocation, reaches a summit of communication in mutual self-giving. A basic criterion of chastity is the truthfulness of love in their communication. Man and woman 'reveal' themselves to each other in their relationships, and especially in the conjugal act if this is in harmony with all of their daily-life 'togetherness'.

Speaking here of sexuality we should not think merely of genitality. Womanhood and manhood have their imprint in all the dimensions of physical, psychic and spiritual expressions and experiences. However, sexuality is to be understood neither as the chief identification of the human person nor as a kind of addition. It comes to its fullness and truth through integration with all the other dimensions and relationships. Much depends on how we recognize and honour the equal dignity and complementarity of man and woman as gift of God.

The quality of the relationship between married couples in their whole life, as well as in the expressions of intimacy, deter-

F

mines to a great extent as well the dialogue between the parents and children, with their differing tonalities: father-son, father-daughter, mother-son, mother-daughter. The father, enriched by conjugal love, communicates as father even without explicit words. The child understands this fatherly, manly language even before he or she can grasp his words. Equally, and probably even more, the child needs the motherly dialogue expressed in tenderness, constant readiness, intuitive understanding, playfulness. Happy the child who, in this multiform dialogue with father and mother, is reaping the harvest of a harmonious and rich dialogue between the parents.

Even celibacy for the kingdom of God is greatly indebted to the multi-dimensional dialogue between mother and father and parents and children, without which young people would never have reached that level which allows them to love with a Christ-like love even those who otherwise are unloved. Consecrated celibacy by no means implies a sort of renunciation of manhood or womanhood. Although those who have grasped and freely chosen celibacy for the sake of the Lord renounce genital-sexual satisfaction, all their other means of communication — verbal and non-verbal — are marked by the complementarity and reciprocity between man and woman that is part of God's design for humankind.

Of itself, bi-sexuality points towards marriage — however, not by necessity but by free choice. In God's intention marriage, as sacrament of salvation, is as much a vocation as celibacy. It becomes vocation in reality if the young person, before God, searches where he or she can best develop the precious capacities to love faithfully and to serve the well-being and salvation of others. Marriage is the ordinary way, while celibacy, by free choice, is a response to a special calling by God and to the special needs of others. This does not mean, however, that it is something extraordinary for young people to ask themselves whether this might be for them the appropriate way. On the contrary, it would be less than normal and a sign of underdevelopment if the young Christian never posed the explicit question.

The free choice of celibacy for the kingdom of God is a helpful witness for those who, despite their original intention, remain celibate because they are unable to marry, or have not found the appropriate partner or have been abandoned by their spouse. This condition can be a crucial crossroads at the beginning, but it can also become just as much a fulfilment vocation and road to holiness as for those whose first choice has been celibacy for the kingdom of God.

Both the way of marriage and the way of celibacy have their joys and noble chances, but both also require a 'Yes' to the following of Christ crucified and the renunciation and fight against all forms of selfishness. Only thus can people develop their manhood or womanhood and reach their genuine capacity to love as 'sexed' persons and to love far beyond the sexual dimensions.

Sexuality has its full and truthful expression and language in bodily union only in marriage. Only there, consecrated for indissoluble love and fidelity, are the two partners in truth 'one flesh'. Sexual intercourse outside marriage does bring together temporarily two sexual bodies, but it does not make two *persons* 'one flesh'. However, in marriage as in other states of life, there are various degrees of approximation and alienation in fidelity and love. For the redeemed, therefore, aiming towards fullness of truthfulness and faithfulness is indispensable in this vocation just as in the rest of moral and religious life.

Next to the choice of state, the choice of husband or wife is one of the great decisions of life. The following criteria should be seriously considered: Can I hope that, if I choose this partner, we will go together, in mutual support, on the road of salvation and holiness? Does this choice arise from a love that comes from God and leads to God? Can I realistically hope that with this person we will be able to keep the covenant of fidelity in good and difficult times 'until death do us part'? Does this choice promise a rich and fruitful dialogue, including intimacy, favourable to our growth in truthfulness and love? Can I reasonably hope that this partner will be a good *parent* of the hoped-for children?

Truthfulness is a decisive criterion of the authenticity of all expressions of love by words, signs and bodily intimacy. Hence, on the road to marriage and in the choice of a partner, all words and signs which awaken false hopes are to be avoided. The road that finally leads to the covenant of faithfulness must be marked by honesty and sincerity.

One of the most relevant consequences of this principle of absolute truthfulness is that sexual intercourse, in the sense of the profound mutual gift and the biblical 'knowing each other' — Adam *knew* Eve — is unthinkable outside the marriage covenant. Extramarital and premarital intercourse is not a truly conjugal experience.

All too frequently a man requests with passionate oaths of love and faithfulness, his girl friend's total bodily surrender. "We consider ourselves as married"! But soon after, having got what he wanted, he declares, "I do love you, but I cannot marry you" — for this or that reason. Time and again I have heard, in parlour and confessional, the sad story of these 'experiences' which are surrounded by a thousand lying assurances of love forever. Of course, we have to distinguish from these the infrequent case of an engaged couple who, only because of external difficulties, are hindered from celebrating their marriage. While we cannot approve their decision to take up a kind of conjugal life without yet being married, we should be fair enough to recognize that here, subjectively, there can be sincerity.

The truthful expression of mutuality of two persons who are created in the image of God implies the recognition of the equal dignity of woman and man. Assertions by word or behaviour that woman is inferior to man contradict the truth that both, in their mutuality, are created in the image of God. Or more concretely, we can say that a man who looks down on woman as inferior does not act according to his dignity as image of God; he is unfaithful to his own dignity and vocation. If equal dignity is fully acknowledged, then their diversity is mutually enriching. Truthful love says in its whole conduct: "It is good that you are; it is good that you are *thus* . . ." Both man and woman are at their best on the road towards the full realization of their high dignity and mutuality as image and likeness of God for each other.

How said it is that in today's world we have to insist that sexuality is not a consumer good! It is a great evil that many people are so marked as consumers that this prevalent trait infiltrates even their relationships with the other sex and their own sexuality. Wherever the other is desired as object for the satisfaction of one's own lust, sexuality is degraded by clouds of lies and deceptions. Then it becomes cheap, trivial, a source of sadness and nausea. For people who are slaves to senseless consumption in almost all of their life, there is little chance to learn the chaste language of truthful love. But those who keep the scale of values, while enjoying life and its gifts, are also better prepared to reap a rich harvest of joy in their sexual love and in their capacity to renounce whatever contradicts true love.

In an environment in which an anti-baby attitude is virulent, only a great and truthful conjugal and parental love can give a convincing witness. Conjugal love is the only abiding source of generous, responsible parenthood. "Conjugal love is fully human, exclusive and open for the transmission of life" (*The Christian Family*, 29).

What our world needs most are holy couples with the beauty and strength of conjugal and parental love, side by side with Christians who, for the sake of the heavenly kingdom, have renounced marriage and are able to love the unloved who are most in need of them.

Marriage and celibacy are a great challenge for Christians who live in a superficial and truthless environment. The transparence and integrity of the relationship between man and woman are not possible without the grace of God who is the source of all truth and love; and this has to be acknowledged constantly in humble prayer and thanksgiving. Those who listen together to the word of God, treasure it in their hearts and meditate on it together will best be able to accept each other as gift of God and to travel together on the road to ever more truthfulness, faithfulness and love.

In all of life, but particularly in the field of chastity, aiming at sheer mediocrity is doomed to failure. On the other hand, those who have consolidated their fundamental option for the road of holiness need never be fainthearted. Even if they experience how far they are behind the full ideal, they should not be discouraged. God sees the good will and blesses it.

*   *   *

Gracious Father, we adore your design in creating man and woman in your image and likeness. We praise you for redeeming us in all our dimensions. Help us in our state of life to become for each other ever more an image of your love which is stronger than all the love of men and more tender than the love of mothers.

Grant to your church and to the world of today holy families. Guide and illumine young people in the choice of their state of life. Help them to find their vocation, whether for marriage or for celibacy for your kingdom. Strengthen and console those who, despite their original choice, have to live celibacy.

Come to the help of married couples in crises, so that they can fully accept each other, pardon each other, bear the burden of each other and grow in love.

Fill us with your love and truth so that we can be chaste in all our relationships and grow together in the capacity to love the poorest, those unloved and estranged.

CHAPTER FOURTEEN

Life entrusted to loving responsibility

"No one of us lives, and equally no one of us dies, for himself alone. If we live, we live for the Lord; and if we die, we die for the Lord. Whether therefore we live or die, we belong to the Lord. This is why Christ died and came to life again, to establish his lordship over dead and living" (Rom 14:7–9).

"I have come that men may have life, and may have it in fullness. I am the good shepherd; the good shepherd lays down his life for the sheep. The hireling, when he sees the wolf coming, abandons the sheep and runs away, because he is no shepherd and the sheep are not his" (Jn 10:11–12).

FOR the Christian, bodily life is not the highest good for which all other values may be sacrificed; but to give one's life in the service of one's neighbour is the supreme possibility of love (cf. Jn 15:13). Thus the tree of Christ's cross becomes the tree of life. Christ gives his life so that his friends may have fullness of life.

Inherent in this fullness of life is the readiness to expose health and life to necessary risks, when it is a matter of serving others and to do so in the discipleship of Christ. Since life is a precious good from God, this willingness deserves Jesus' praise. That is why he expresses thanks in the morning prayer of his life: "Thou hast prepared for me a body. Whole-offerings and sin-offerings thou didst not delight in. Then I said, 'Here am I: as it is written of me in the scroll, I have come, O God, to do thy will' " (Heb 10:5–7).

There are all too many people today who want to give legal status to the 'art' of sacrificing the innocent life of others in order to make their own life more comfortable. We hear boasting about progress in freedom and privacy which allows mothers and doctors to sacrifice millions of children in their mother's womb year by year, in order to diminish the guests at the table of life or to prevent the burden of children who might be handicapped.

We can imagine with what wrath German soldiers, who had buried many of their friends, heard propaganda minister Goebbels say: "The fertile regions of the Don and Kuban are worth the lives of German soldiers!" This has been the way of thinking and acting by war 'heroes' and warmongers throughout history. The sacrifice of thousands of civilians in Nagasaki and Hiroshima was excused with the spurious argument that it saved the lives of thousands of American soldiers. In reality these were hecatombs to the moloch-ideology of imposed 'unconditional surrender' of the enemy, such as were offered so often in past history. Millions of 'undesired' people were thrown by Hitler into the jaws of a myth of a superior race, just as other millions were sacrificed by Stalin in adoration of his dialectic materialism. And the most horrifying aspect is that they easily found willing collaborators.

These events of ancient and recent history must shake the consciences of all decent people. They have to ask themselves what to do in order to prevent similar sacrifices to the devouring false gods of the future. A Christian, who believes in the Good Shepherd and accepts his supreme commandment of love of God and neighbour as a rule of life, must face these questions unequivocally and also try to acquire competence in this continuing battle for worldwide respect for human life.

Not only our own but also our neighbour's life, indeed the lives of all people are entrusted to our shared responsibility. In a world in which people's needs cry to us from everywhere and where we can exercise worldwide influence, we would be following the bad example of the priest and levite in the biblical parable if we did not care for the life and health of other people. With sacrifices no greater than those of the merciful Samaritan we can rescue many who have fallen into the hands of 'robbers'.

If Christians were to spend as much on healing lepers as they spend on the damaging use of nicotine and alcohol, the plague of leprosy — which at the present time has about thirty million people in its grip — could be quickly wiped out. Is this too much to ask from people who believe in their vocation to holiness? Even those who are not slaves to any life-damaging addiction should, in thanksgiving, spend generously for those to be rescued.

I stand before each of my readers as a beggar for lepers. In many parts of the world I have seen their suffering. In each diocese or at least in each country, there is a church institution collecting help for the healing of lepers and the prevention of leprosy. But the funds should flow more generously to these works.

Hundreds of millions of people suffer starvation, and millions of lives are threatened each year by hunger. They stretch out their arms to us for urgent help, indeed for generous help.

The crusades against planned abortion, against war and mass starvation must go hand in hand; otherwise we would not be coherent and credible. Those protesting loudly against the threat of nuclear weapons, which can destroy the whole of humankind, do well. But all, while protesting against spectacular evils, should ask themselves if they are willing also to make their personal contribution in the fight against dangerous hunger and contagious diseases, or to involve themselves politically for more generous help for the poorest countries. Are they, indeed, even caring for their own and their near neighbours' health? I think, for instance, of the guilt feelings of many lung-cancer patients and larynxectomized men and women who were heavy smokers, and of the conviction of many doctors that smokers polluting the air are sometimes the cause of such damage to others.

Competent and generous development helpers and medical missionaries are the merciful samaritans of today. During a course in a poor area of Africa I met two young Italian women, medical doctors, assisting there. I was told that originally they had obliged themselves for only a few years, but seeing the tremendous misery and need, they prolonged their stay, time and again, finally realizing that this meant nothing less than giving up the chance to marry and to have children. They have saved many lives. We could do something similar without such a high price just by making a generous offering for the great needs, offerings which in many cases can be lifesaving.

Capital punishment is a 'life' subject. There were and are still two opposing opinions in the church. Some — especially fundamentalists — justify the death penalty by quotes from the

Old Testament. Others oppose it by insisting on the revelation of God's mercy in the New Testament and by pointing to the fundamental truth that Christ died on the cross for us sinners who might have deserved eternal punishment.

Since my earliest writings as a moral theologian I have opposed, on principle, the death penalty. I am convinced, at least on principle, that this is more in keeping with the compassionate love of Christ and the heavenly Father for sinners. But besides that, there are historical reasons. I think especially of the German state under Hitler, one of the greatest mass-murderers. Although the juridical successors are not to be accused of these official crimes against life, they would do well to remember the facts and humbly to abstain from killing people found guilty by fallible human judges.

Although these reasons are not so stringent in other countries, it cannot be denied that even in such democratic countries as the USA, the lives of black people and other minorities were often taken while people of the ruling class got away with disproportionate or no punishment. In general, we can assert that there is such a shameful human tradition of judicial murder by states that it is best to break away totally from this tradition and to concentrate instead on preventive measures and rehabilitation.

However, this is an area where different opinions have existed and still exist within the church, and we should be tolerant of others who think differently. But one thing must be vigorously asserted: a state which refuses to protect the innocent life of the unborn can claim no legitimacy for passing death penalties, since the only good reason for the death penalty is protection of innocent life against violence.

*   *   *

O God, Creator of all life, you seek not the death of the sinner but his conversion so that he may live fully. We all live by your generosity and mercy. We thank you for the wonderful gift of being, to which you have added the promise of eternal sharing in your life and bliss. You have called all people to eternal life. Help us through your grace to assist each other on our road to fullness of being and eternal life.

We praise you, Father, for havinng sent us the Good

Shepherd who has laid down his life and thus has shown us the sublime opportunity to love our neighbours in the service of life, justice and peace. Make us witnesses to our faith and hope in the resurrection of the body.

Merciful God, since earliest times men like Cain have murdered their brothers and sisters in time of peace and even more in time of war, thus terribly dishonouring your name as Father of all. We grieve especially because so often even Christians, who call you 'our Father', have neglected and even defied your mandate to serve and save life, thus sinning at least through inactivity or complicity. Before your judgement we all must humbly ask ourselves if we have shown gratitude for the gift of life by a wise and generous shared responsibility for the life and health of our fellowmen.

Forgive us, Father, for having damaged our own life and that of others by an unreasonable, unhealthy life-style. Make us signs of healing goodness and peace, heralds of non-violent commitment to peace and justice.

CHAPTER FIFTEEN

Health and holiness

"John too was informed of all this by his disciples. Summoning two of their number he sent them to the Lord with this message: 'Are you the one who is to come, or are we to expect some other?' . . . There and then (Jesus) cured many sufferers from diseases, plagues and evil spirits; and on many blind people he bestowed sight. Then he gave them his answer: 'Go' he said 'and tell John what you have seen and heard: how the blind recover their sight, the lame walk, the lepers are made clean, the deaf hear, the dead are raised to life, the poor are hearing the good news — and happy is the man who does not find me a stumbling-block' " (Lk 7 : 18–23).

HOLY scripture leaves no doubt that healing the sick is an essential dimension of Christ's mission. Sometimes it seems that for him, on some occasions, healing is more urgent than preaching the good news. Or rather, healing the sick is a privileged form of proclaiming the good news of the messianic time. He heals on the sabbath although he knows that this makes him a stumbling-block for the legalists.

The sermon on the plain is introduced by this remark: "Everyone in the crowd was trying to touch him, because power went out from him and cured them all" (Lk 6 : 19). Healing is a manifestation not only of Jesus' power but, above all, of his compassionate love. He somehow sees in disease an aspect of the powers of evil, a sign of a world in need of redemption and liberation. Healing the sick is also a symbol of the healing of those with broken hearts. Yet Jesus rejects vigorously the common opinion of the Middle East at that time which adjudged the sick and/or their parents as cursed because of their sins (cf. Jn 9 : 22). Especially lepers had to suffer severely under this superstition. They were outcast, untouchable and despised as the most miserable sinners. Jesus reached out to them, healed them and reintegrated them into society, restored them their religious and civil honour.

By his healing activities Jesus glorifies the Father. But he also shows us patient suffering as one way of following him on the way of the cross. However, acceptance of suffering and illness in ourselves and others has a positive meaning only if we do everything possible to heal what can be healed.

Modern medicine has won many battles against disease and will win many more. Yet at the same time the modern world, with its unhealthy life-style and its reckless abuse and destruction of the environment, has opened the floodgates for legions of evils. This warns us that we should not simply resign ourselves to sickness as if it were sent by God; we should beware of blaming God for the many evils which sinful man has produced in sinful ways.

Nevertheless, while doing our best to heal what can be healed and removing the causes of sickness where they can be removed, we can patiently take upon ourselves in shared responsibility the burden of what cannot be healed, just as Jesus took upon his shoulders the cross which human iniquity had prepared for him. We may detest all sins, including those which have disordered our world and caused diseases, but at the same time we can bear our cross in time of illness. We would not be true disciples of Christ if we cursed our sufferings. Our just rebellion against the sinful causes of evil must never become rebellion against God who, in time of sickness, gives us strength and puts us to the test.

When we raise the important question of what health has to do with salvation and holiness, we first must try to clarify the concept of human health.

Health is not the same as capacity to work, although this is very desirable. Health is equally more than exuberant bodily strength, especially when the higher capacities such as the search for truth and ultimate meaning are neglected.

Human health can be defined as the greatest possible embodiment of the spirit and the noblest spiritualization of the bodily dimension. There can be a surplus of physical vitality but a pitiful lack of openness to the spirit and to healthy human relations. On the other hand, a physically suffering body can make transparent the spirit of goodness, joy, peace, compassion and serenity. A well-trained body is an excellent thing if it submits to the higher values.

The integrity of the body and its organs is a precious good entrusted to our personal and shared responsibility. But this is far from being human wholeness and health. On the one hand there are ways of risking health which do violence to wholeness and our vocation to holiness. Conversely, there can be generous commitments involving substantial risk to physical health, which are genuine expressions of the pursuit of holiness in the service of neighbour and the common good.

Of great relevance for wholeness, salvation and the service of salvation is *psychic* health. But even here we have to be cautious in our evaluation. While writing this I am informed of the death of a dear friend, a genial man in many respects. As a result of shocking experiences during Hitler's war, a depressive predisposition caused him a nervous breakdown. He suddenly began to cry out loudly against the war crimes of Hitler; only the psychiatrist could save him from being executed. Later we talked often about his situation which he could analyse sharply. Thanks to modern medicine it could be kept under control; but what helped him more than the drugs was his astonishing serenity and conformity with God's will. Beyond and above the psychic illness there was a feeling and force of wholeness which allowed him to accept and transcend his handicap.

Psychosomatic medicine, psychoanalysis and the various schools of psychotherapy have revolutionized the concepts of health, sickness and healing. Attention centres largely on the phenomenon of neuroses. There, precious energies are blocked by unfavourable conditions in the environment, by disturbed human relationships and by unresolved personal problems. They are not properly discovered or cultivated, yet they are not dead. So long as they do not find their healthy dynamics, they turn inward, causing tensions and strange reactions. However, it would be a great error and injustice to denigrate persons suffering neuroses or to inflict moral condemnations on them. The neurosis should be understood as a cry from the depths for inner wholeness and healthy relationships, a cry for someone who can help to discover these inner forces and their meaningful application.

Victor Frankl, the father of logotherapy, has drawn our

attention to *noogenic* neurosis which develops in an existential vacuum when the inborn desire for ultimate meaning is frustrated. The conscious and frequently unconscious loss of meaning or the repression of the search for meaning, disturbs the whole somatic and psychic health. The disharmony between achievement or pleasure-seeking and the lack of search for a scale of values affects the person in all his or her dimensions and relationships. Healing requires a new impetus in the search for meaning and the gradual realization of the level of meaning which insight provides. Here we see the insoluble relation between health and wholeness-holiness.

The experiences of logotherapists suggest that everyone who, respectfully and patiently helps his or her neighbour in the search for meaning, exercises a precious therapy in an indispensable perspective of redemption. Persons who are physically or psychically sick or handicapped are most seriously threatened in their wholeness and salvation if they fail to search for the meaning of life or refuse to find an acceptable meaning for their suffering. The winning of a convincing value which fills heart and mind is a great gain on the road to human health.

There are two extreme positions. Thomas à Kempis, in his *Imitation of Christ*, thinks that nobody becomes holier through illness, while St Hildegard says that "God's dwelling place is normally not in a healthy body". Both expressions have to be evaluated in their context. Nobody should put off striving for holiness until he is sick (Thomas à Kempis); and nobody should doubt that, with God's help, illness or any kind of suffering can be an opportunity on the road to holiness. St Hildegard insists with St Paul: "Power comes to its full strength in weakness" (2 Cor 12:9). But she also rightly warns that nobody should weaken his or her health by imprudent asceticism or an unhealthy style of life. God does not promise special help if we imprudently and irresponsibly jeopardize our physical or psychic wholeness.

The tireless fight against sin, the striving for holiness and especially a profound experience of God's purifying fire can deeply shake a person in need of thorough-going purification. But it is equally true that a trustful discipleship of Christ and the experience of God's nearness and love produce wonderful energies for building wholeness and human health in all its dimensions. Inner peace and unshakable serenity, God's gifts for those who seek only to conform with his will, give astonishing strength to bear with life's tasks and tests. The inner harmony, reflecting the union with God, is a blessing also for bodily and psychic health.

The great physician Viktor von Weizsäcker tells us that "illness is a mode of being human." Man has to pass through the experience of weakness, unhealthiness and death on the road to eternal life. If we accept God's design as well as we can understand it in the various situations of life, then even grave suffering and illness can become times of grace. Illness reminds us of the finiteness and frailty of earthly life, and challenges us not to lose sight of life immortal with God. Thus it is an offer and a chance for deeper reflection and clearer direction towards our abiding vocation. We have to see both danger and opportunity in illness. In the school of the Crucified it is an opportunity for the friends of Christ.

*   *   *

Protect us, O Lord, from all sin and self-destruction. Heal us, for we have sinned against you and against our own wholeness. Grant that a healthy soul may dwell in our body and radiate purity and peace, whether our body be weak or strong.

Grant us a deeper insight into the meaning of life, health and unhealthiness. But, above all, bestow on us that love which guarantees that everything — suffering and ill-health included — can turn out for our good.

Give us insight, grace and strength to care more for salvation and holiness than for health, and yet to care enough for health not to impair our striving for holiness and generous service.

Gracious God, assist and console the sick. Illumine and heal those poor and plagued persons who have gravely failed in searching for the true meaning of life and, as consequence, are sick in body and soul. Send them loving and competent people to guide them in a renewed yearning for a meaningful life.

CHAPTER SIXTEEN

Dying with Christ

"The truth is, Christ was raised to life . . . In Christ all will be brought to life; but each in his own proper place: Christ the firstfruits, and afterwards, at his coming, those who belong to Christ. Then comes the end, when he delivers up the kingdom to the Father, after abolishing every kind of domination, authority and power. For he is destined to reign until God has put all enemies under his feet; and the last enemy to be abolished is death. . . .

"When our mortality has been clothed with immortality, then the saying of Scripture will come true: 'Death is swallowed up; victory is won!' 'O Death, where is your victory? O Death, where is your sting?' The sting of death is sin, and sin gains its power from the law; but, God be praised, he gives us the victory through our Lord Jesus Christ" (1 Cor 15:20–26; 15:54–57).

"For, as I passionately hope, I shall have no cause to be ashamed, but shall speak so boldly that now as always the greatness of Christ will shine out clearly in my person, whether through my life or through my death. For to me life is Christ, and death gain; but what if my living on in the body may serve some good purpose? Which then am I to choose? I cannot tell. I am torn two ways: what I should like is to depart and be with Christ; that is better by far; but for your sake there is greater need for me to stay on in the body" (Phil 1:20–24).

DEATH is surely our abiding neighbour. We live on the road to death, whether we like it or not. It is better to like it, but at least we have to take it fully into account.

Christians who consciously live by faith are different from their unbelieving neighbours. They are familiar with Brother Death. They know its awesomeness, but they have the promises and the firm hope that, by God's grace, their faithful 'Yes' to their vocation to holiness will make the day of their death the feast of the harvest, final fulfilment, victory through Christ, the last 'Yes, here I am'; the homecoming.

Whoever intends to repress the thought of death is doomed to an unreal way of existence, devoid of life's final truth, swimming in the stream of masses who do not want to know where they are going. And anyone who plans his life-programme as if death would not wait for him is more 'under the law of death' than he suspects. The 'repressed' death, dwelling and rebelling in the half-conscious and unconscious layers of the person who attempts this hopeless flight, will play its sinister and befouling role in all that he or she does. The stubborn intention not to face death and not to accept it as part of one's truth blocks all accesses to life's truth.

In the apostle's letter to the Philippians we see how the 'Yes' to life, in clear sight of death fully accepted, gives us supreme freedom for true life. Christ himself becomes our life and our joy. Paul's two sayings, 'death is gain' and 'to me life is Christ' are inseparable for us, just as Christ's death and resurrection are inseparable. In the death of the believer, life becomes transparent as life in Christ Jesus.

Whoever affirms the final meaning of life and death as consciously and trustingly as Paul did, will experience the same liberation from slavish fear of death and law. A dying man expressed this beautifully when his doctor was nervously searching for words to tell him that death was near: "Doctor, are you having trouble telling me that I am going to die? Why? All my life I have lived for this day!"

How different is the picture under the 'law of sin and death', of sin-solidarity and flight from God! We see the untruth of the family in which all members agree only on one decision: to deceive the dying father about the seriousness of his situation, in alliance with a doctor who prefers this kind of 'practice'. The priest is called in only after death for a 'ceremony' good for public appearance. Or we see the fate of a notorious adulterer. His wife, whom he constantly betrayed, stands stone-faced at the graveside while another woman throws a stone into the open grave, crying, 'You murderer of my soul!' Sin-solidarity has its last furious cry.

Solidarity in Christ, redemption and liberation leads to the joyous song of praise: "Praised be God who gives us victory through our Lord Jesus Christ!" (1 Cor 15:57). The same song of victory resounds also in the letter to the Romans: "In Christ the life-giving law of the Spirit has set you free from the law of sin and death" (Rom 8:2).

This victory of salvation-solidarity happens time and again in holy families. John, who always thanked God for his 'holy wife', was weeping when he saw that she was dying. He appealed to the Lord: "Did I not always pray to you to let me die before Francisca? What am I without her?" The Lord's response came through the lips of his dying spouse: "But John, how can you complain? Isn't it the Lord's right to decide about the hour of our death?" John stopped his lamentation then and ever after, turning his mind instead to gratitude for having had his wife for so many years on the road to holiness, and for having her as his best preacher even on her deathbed. And at the time of his own death he faithfully put into practice the lesson she had taught him. When he told his eldest son that the hour of death had come, the son reminded him that the rest of the family, who were on their way, would be gathered there in a few hours. The dying father said: "The Lord calls me now; I cannot wait. Give them my greetings; bid them goodbye for me."

Could John and Francisca leave their children and friends a greater heritage than the witness of their faith and saving-solidarity?

The right attitude to illness and death is not only a most personal decision; it is also a basic question of social ethics. The world needs our effort, our witness and wisdom for the liberating truth.

Ivan Illich rightly sees in the 'Yes' to frailty, illness and mortality the foundation of an authentic human health and healthy relationships. It is a matter of shared courage to accept the full truth of all of life's dimensions. Not only the life of individuals but also the shape of public life changes where people walk consciously together in the shadow of death.

This liberty to accept our life day by day as death approaches, and to sense fully this limited earthly life, is anchored in our faith in the resurrection of Christ and in the divine promise of our resurrection. If Christ is truly our life, then the experience of the loving nearness of God and the intimate communion of life with Christ assures us that this community of love cannot end with our death but is designed by God for all eternity.

What a blessing it would be if the lives, actions and words of all men and women in the healing professions were inspired by these fundamental experiences!

In a certain sense death, our mortality, is natural. Our whole biological frame is directed towards growth and gradual decrease, leading naturally one day to death. However, our dying is something totally different from that of plants and animals. It has the character of a decision to be consciously faced.

Yet historically there is something most unnatural in human death — in the death of the sinner. The flood of sin, growing from its poisoned beginnings into a stream of anguish and terror, is not willed by God. The sinner, closing his heart to redemption, making his choice against salvation-solidarity and thereby locking himself into the guilt of sin-solidarity, cannot blame God or nature for the anguish and futility surrounding his death. We can say simply, with scripture, that this death entered into history through sin.

Within the unnaturalness of unredeemed sinfulness it is 'natural' for the sinner to repress the thought of death, to rebel against it, and to suffer the terrible consequences of this flight and rebellion. But the redeemed, who by God's grace built their life on faith in redemption and resurrection, are indeed liberated from the 'law of death' which the sinner chooses. By the power of grace and faith, a real transubstantiation of death occurs. It becomes a redeemed and trustful dying with Christ within the abiding 'life in Christ'.

But herein, we also have to see the tension between the 'already' and the 'not-yet'.

In God's design we are all meant to be liberated from the terrible death which befits the sinner, as sinner: a death which is a sign of solidarity in sin and futility. Christ, accepting the anguish of the most painful and humiliating death on the cross, echoing the anguished cry of sinful humanity, 'My God, my God, why hast thou forsaken me?' has offered himself as redemptive sacrifice in the supreme act of saving-solidarity. He who, by divine mission, is saving-justice and saving-solidarity, he who is without sin has accepted the passover through the red sea of sin-solidarity and its bitter consequences.

We who put our faith in Christ's saving death and resurrection are liberated from death as punishment and final despair. Yet death has still some painful dimensions even for authentic believers. The first is that most of us are not yet fully detached from all sin and living fully in Christ. Pain and the painful experience of separation from loved ones — in God's design a sharing of saving-solidarity with our Redeemer — might also be a final great chance to overcome, with God's grace, this incoherence with our faith. But more important and more consoling for the redeemed who are called to share Christ's redeeming action in the world is that it is somehow 'natural' that they consciously accept the pains of illness and death 'for the life of the world'. It becomes the solidaric passover from death to life, from the cursed death of the unredeemed to the death of the redeemed, the seed that falls to the ground for new and wonderful life.

We keep firm one important truth: for the believer, as such, death is in no way a curse or punishment. Even the painful aspect of knowing that we need further purification enters into the consoling light of the Paschal Mystery. The final transfiguration of death is most apparent in those who accept death, with all its attendant circumstances, as a gracious presence of the giver of eternal life who brings to completion whatever he has begun and favoured throughout these persons' lifetime.

It is one of the most precious experiences of faith to accompany the dying of Christians who give us convincing testimony that 'Christ is my life and death is gain'. For ourselves and those we love, indeed for all believers, we should never stop praying for the undeserved grace of perseverance in God's love. It is also a matter of fundamental saving-solidarity that we help the dying to receive the consolation of the sacraments of faith as frequently as possible, and all the pastoral help that can be offered in time.

Since the kind of death we are to die depends essentially on our fundamental option for either solidarity of salvation or solidarity of evil, we have also to face our coresponsibility for other people's 'unnatural' death and our own risk of unnatural death in any of its various forms and meanings. As active Chirstians we shall do our best to ensure that no one to whom we can reach out will die the terrible death of the 'unredeemed', a death in guilt and alienation, flight or open rebellion. The world needs this commitment as much as it needs commitment to fight for healthier social structures.

We consider here also 'unnatural' death in the medical sense. In the first place we think of the horrible death by suicide or murder. We all have to ask ourselves how many other people may have participated actively or passively in the process of decay that leads to such explosions of unnaturalness.

Penal law speaks of 'manslaughter' when punishable negligence contributes to the unnatural death of others. But it would be a grave error to look only at the definitions and limits of penal law. Negligence can take a thousand forms. Reckless driving is one of the most frequent, but the more than one hundred thousand deaths on our planet's highways each year are far from being all consequences of reckless driving. There is the irresponsibility of the driver who takes 'just one more' drink before driving, the carelessness about upkeep and repair of the car or the roadways, driving in moments of depression, anger or near-exhaustion, and countless other forms of culpable negligence that may lead to death.

Millions of people burn out life's energies and shorten their life-span by immoderate use of alcohol, drugs and tobacco. In their unnaturally early death there is a terrible interplay of collective sin: neglect by parents and educators, by pastors and moral theologians, and by doctors who dare not alert people to their senseless life-style because they do not want to be accused of 'moralism' — while, indeed, their neglect is immoral.

Also immoral would be the judgemental attitude that puts all the blame on those who, for various reasons, die early or violently. Redemption does not allow us simply to point to culprits. Rather, we are to take up our own responsibility generously and examine always our own conscience.

It is a woeful commentary on our times that the trend today, even in medical circles, to accept rather easily the killing of early life in the mother's womb and the foreshortening of the life-span by abuse and unhealthy life-styles has its counterpart in the trend to prolong the irrevocable death-process by highly sophisticated and expensive means, although these manoeuvres benefit neither the unconscious patients nor their families.

This phenomenon is at least partially the result of the 'repressed' thought of death. The enormous efforts and costs wasted on artificial and useless prolongation of the death-process could be better applied to rehabilitation of the handicapped and assistance to families with handicapped children.

While liberation from 'the law of death' categorically excludes suicide and arbitrary abbreviation of one's life-span, it enables us to look serenely towards natural death in conformity with God's will. In this context we have to face today's discussions on euthanasia. In the forming of healthy public opinions, this is one of the debates in which Christians must participate with special competence.

Etymologically, 'euthanasia' means 'dying well'. In a christian understanding this includes: striving for a good life which is the best preparation for a good death, the heartfelt 'Yes' to life and death, loving care for the dying by their families, friends, neighbours and especially by the members of the healing professions, alleviating the sufferings of terminal illness, and bringing the consolation of faith.

An important service which the church owes its sick members is to console and strengthen them with the sacraments while they are still able to receive them in full consciousness. The anointing of the sick should never be deferred until the last moment. It is not a sacrament only for the dying but equally for the sick who desire and hope for recovery and a fruitful passing-through the time of illness.

In today's medical-ethical discussions, euthanasia means: a) the refusal of helpful measures in order to speed up the coming of death; b) the application of measures intended to cause death directly.

The church's Magisterium and theologians categorically condemn both modalities of euthanasia. It is an attack on God's sovereignty over death and life. Consciously to cause one's own death, to call others to be cooperators in suicide or to refuse helpful means to which the dying or gravely ill person is entitled are arbitrary acts and by no means a liberation. If death-speeding methods are applied without the consent of the sick person and with the explicit intention to cause death, this, of course, simply, is murder. Only under the barbarous régime of Hitler was this merciless 'mercy-killing' called 'euthanasia'.

In the sense of a) refusal of helpful treatment with the

purpose of shortening life or b) direct measures to speed up death, euthanasia is not only a moral problem but also, in our times, a problem of legislation. We do not ask the state to put under penal sanctions all transgressions of ethical principles; but legalizing euthanasia, or a legal declaration that the state leaves such decisions to privacy, is a betrayal of the state's specific duty. Its duty is to protect the weak and the aged, the sick and the handicapped, to protect the sacredness of human life.

It is easy to foresee what effects a legalization of euthanasia would produce. All those who burden their fellowmen or the state would constantly feel to question themselves if now was not the proper time to disappear from the theatre of life — by euthanasia. The indispensable trust in doctors would be undermined if the medical profession were to agree to such legislation and show willingness to kill ailing people on request. The argument that legalization is proposed only for those who freely request it does not hold. As soon as euthanasia were to be legalized, many people would begin to feel unjust pressures and many gates would be opened for manipulation.

Quite different is the application of heavy pain-killers or the courageous attempt to save life by unusual means when ordinary means have failed, with the risk of abbreviating the life unintentionally. These do not fall under the concept of euthanasia which we radically reject.

Another matter which concerns each of us personally, and is highly relevant for Christians who participate in the formation of public opinions, is the right of the patients — especially of the terminally ill — to be truthfully informed about their situation. Truthfulness is essential for healthy personal relationships and for healthy communities. It has special relevance in the patient-doctor relationship.

Of course, an unfavourable diagnosis is not a truth that can always be communicated nakedly and at once to the sick person. Not to give all the facts at once is not at all a lie if the intention is to tell the truth step by step in the best possible graduality. Doctors, nurses and members of the family can tactfully probe to what extent the patient is ready to hear the full truth and to help prepare the next step. It is best for the patient to help the doctor by showing his readiness and courage to face the truth. When it was a question of the reappearance of my larynx-cancer

I told the doctor emphatically that I support the principle, 'Only truth can liberate us'. I saw how the doctor immediately felt at ease and did not hesitate to explain the facts.

In many African tribes I heard that a chief is told only what he wants to hear; he is not told unpleasant facts if he prefers not to hear them. But if he gives clear signs that always and under all circumstances he desires full information, then he will never be deceived. This widespread cultural phenomenon is quite understandable but it does not correspond to the christian concept of frankness. Gradual communication of a serious diagnosis, especially of terminal illness, can be a high art of love and truthfulness in a dynamic process of interpersonal relationships and constant openness. But it is simply unacceptable to tell lies only because the patient is not ready here and now for the full truth; he or she has to be helped to prepare him/herself.

What would it mean if doctors and members of the family followed the principle, "You should tranquillize the patient by lies as long as possible"? Then there would be no means to free the patient from distrust and suspicion. Even the most favourable diagnosis would not find trust, and communication would become more and more meaningless.

In recent years there have been discussions world wide, about taking healthy organs from corpses, immediately after death, and transferring them to ailing people who are in need. Legislators who are to consider this matter have to choose between two possibilities: either to allow doctors generally to make life-saving use of organs of the deceased as soon as death is certain (unless there is an explicit protest by a will or by family members), or to invite people to make their will in time to arrange for the use of the organs after death.

The second solution seems the more ideal if a sufficient number of people thus extend, beyond their death, their generous responsibility for the life and health of others by encouraging the use of their organs. But I also see no serious objections against the first solution when this finds agreement in public opinion and actually helps to save more lives.

*　　　　*　　　　*

We praise you and thank you, Lord Jesus Christ, for having conquered sin-solidarity through your death and resurrection, and having introduced all who believe in you into saving-solidarity which gives a new meaning to the death of believers. We thank you for having done everything to free us from the law of anguished death.

Each time we take the cup of salvation we praise and proclaim your death and resurrection until you come through Brother Death to take us home into the eternal kingdom of the Father.

We pray for the grace of perseverance in your love, and a happy death for ourselves and for all people, whereby we finally can entrust our life into your hands.

Holy Mary, Mother of God, pray for us sinners, now and at the hour of our death.

CHAPTER SEVENTEEN

Ecological responsibility

"So God created man in his own image; in the image of God he created him; male and female he created them. God blessed them and said to them, 'Be fruitful and increase, fill the earth and subdue it, rule over the fish in the sea, the birds of heaven, and every living thing that moves upon the earth.' God also said, 'I give you all plants that bear seed everywhere on earth, and every tree bearing fruit which yield seed: they shall be yours for food. All green plants I give for food to the wild animals, to all the birds of heaven, and to all the reptiles on earth, every living creature.' So it was; and God saw all that he had made, and it was very good. . . .

"Then the Lord God planted a garden in Eden away to the east, and there he put the man whom he had formed. The Lord God made trees spring from the ground, all trees pleasant to look at and good for food; and in the middle of the garden he set the tree of life and the tree of the knowledge of good and evil" (Gen 1:27–31; 2:8–9).

FORTY years ago nobody would have expected in a treatise on moral theology or spirituality a chapter on ecological responsibility; only a new world situation and new knowledge have brought this dimension to the foreground. It has become a central problem of human and christian responsibility in and for the world.

This does not imply, however, that we have nothing to learn in the field from Christians of the past. Let us remember St Francis of Assisi and his loving respect for animals and plants, the sun and moon. He discovered in them a loving word of the Father in heaven; they invited him to see them as part of the great choir of praise to God. In St Alphonsus' beautiful book on *The Art of Loving Jesus,* the first part, 'Love calls for Love', records his admiration of how, in all the created reality, God

107

reveals his beauty and goodness and speaks to us his language of loving care. And he quotes many saints who understood the 'language' of the world around them as a constant invitation to love and to praise God not only with words but also through the right attitude towards all of creation.

The saints combine the spirit of praise and of reverence for God's gifts with a temperance that forbids their idolizing creatures or becoming their slaves. This basic attitude is more effective in the long run than mere principles and laws for the protection of ecological balance.

If the world of today were to return to the spirit of praise found in the psalms, in the whole Bible and in all authentic disciples of Christ, it would not be too difficult to resolve the ecological crisis of which we are to speak here. They have taught us a redeemed and redeeming relationship with all of creation, together with a saving solidarity with all of humankind in our own times and with all the generations to come.

The two accounts of creation in the first two chapters of Genesis are highly relevant for the right understanding of the relations between humankind and nature. Both accounts speak of God's loving care for his privileged human creature, but also his joy in all the created reality and his solicitude for all living creatures.

God has given man no right to feel entitled to exploit nature. He wills that man, in his attitude towards his environment, be in the image of God who wants his creation to be and to remain 'very good'. Man is to 'subdue' the earth as a faithful steward of the Creator.

By entrusting the wonderful garden of Eden to man, God does, indeed, give man a tremendous advance of trust but no right whatsoever to act arbitrarily or ruthlessly with other creatures. If man entrusts himself to God and accepts his clear guidance to celebrate the sabbath in order to be and to remain an adorer in all his life and in all his relationships, then he surely will not lack a spirit of discernment and responsibility towards his environment.

Several modern writers try to blame not only Christians and Christendom for reckless treatment of the human environment but even holy scripture which Christians consider as divine revelation. For their purpose they distort the word 'subdue' out of its context and read into the text an orientation towards a one-sided 'knowledge of domination'.

It is true that the prevailing 'knowledge of dominaion' and the exploitation of nature in modern science, technology, economics and politics are main causes of the sad ecological situation. It can also be agreed that holy scripture favoured a rational attitude towards the material world, the plants and animals, and contributed partially to the development of modern science and technology in the western world. But a reasonable and rational attitude and a meaningful knowledge of domination are one thing; a quite different thing is to put knowledge of domination and control in the first place and to neglect the knowledge of wholeness and salvation. If the modern world has taken the latter course, it has been contrary to what scripture and the lives of the saints have taught and still teach us.

The God of the Bible is the Creator who blesses his work and teaches humanity about the pre-eminence of salvation truth and salvation knowledge. This includes the responsibility of humankind for the wholeness of persons, for good human relationships and care for a healthy world.

Even when man had sinned and when the world was flooded by streams of human sins and sinful traditions, God was taking care not only of the just man, Noah, and his descendants but also of all the species of animals, the clean and the so-called 'unclean'. It is true that, in the covenant with Noah, man is now entitled to eat the meat of animals — but under the condition that man imitates God in the preservation of the animal world (cf. Genesis, 7–9).

The Christians of today, who take seriously the mission 'You are the salt of the earth', become well informed about the complex ecological problems in order to exercise their influence responsibly and to make their contribution towards shaping public opinions and important political decisions in this field.

There are three qualities necessary if Christians are to have a healthy impact on the ecological problems. First, they have to be adorers in spirit and truth; secondly, they should be gifted with wisdom and discernment; thirdly, they should be creative in an affirmative sense. This creativity allows a prudent manipulation of the given material of one's environment. We do not encroach on the limits of our mandate to subdue the earth when we decipher the dynamics of the biological and other processes or when we use our knowledge and skill to transform them in a way that helps people and harms no one.

We cannot even imagine our gardens, our agriculture, our capacity to feed six billion people without selective breeding, without irrigating arid land. Man does well to clear the jungles in the right proportions, and to multiply the harvest by chemical fertilizer. He is praiseworthy when he lays out wonderful parks and gardens, for even after the fall it remains true that God has entrusted the earth to man as a wonderful garden, "the garden of Eden to till it and to care for it" (Gen 2 : 15). Nothing can be said against man's skill and planning in mining minerals used for the many goals of economy and art. But all this has to be done with wisdom and care, so that the harmony of the innumerable ecological factors, which allow a healthy life, will not be destroyed.

Today's highly-developed scientific and technological man comes closer and closer to limits which may not be trespassed without endangering our spaceship, Earth, which might become uninhabitable through man's fault. No powerful nation and no 'élite' of scientists and technologists have the right to take risks which might have deleterious effects from which the whole of humankind and all future generations might suffer greatly. Irreversible mistakes can be made by unwise pioneering in a field about which we do not yet know the complex interplay.

The earth is part of an interaction between the sun and all the planets, and the sun-system itself moves and develops in a not-yet-well-known interplay with all the other factors of the universe. On earth, billions of factors in the most complex interplay constitute the biosphere, the milieu of human life.

This interaction is already seriously disturbed for instance, by the waste of irreplaceable minerals, especially fossil energy-resources, by the pollution of water and air. Billions of fish, destined by the Creator for all humankind by reproducing themselves for all generations, die because of water pollution caused by various poisons from industrial wastes. The margin of tolerance of ionizing radiation by industry and armaments has been exceeded in many parts of the world. Asbestos is produced and used in increasing quantities, although it is now known as a principal cause of cancer, second only to excessive smoking.

The recent stupendous progress in research of recombinant DNA might be a blessing in the field of medicine and genetics; it might open new horizons for selective breeding of plants, cereals, animals and so on; but it might also produce irresistible viruses and endanger the genetic heritage.

The most threatening aspect in this whole situation, however, is that modern man has invested his energies one-sidedly in knowledge of domination and exploitation, while allowing himself terrible under-development in wisdom and discernment. Can humanity hope to face the ecological crisis if this disproportion continues to determine the programmes of our educational systems, our politics and our economics?

The technologically highly-developed countries of East and West are the main causes of the disturbed biosphere and eco-sphere. If the countries of the so-called Third World were to follow the same quantitative growth mania and excessive waste in consumption and armaments, humanity would not be far from a total ecological collapse.

The main culprits and profiteers in this picture of ecological damage are also the outspoken enemies of a worldwide effort to raise people's consciousness of the situation and to form an ecological conscience. The armies of scientists, employed by the armament industries and their allies, are ordered to deceive the people who are becoming aware of the grave ecological dangers.

But many of us have to ask ourselves, sincerely and humbly, if we are not somehow among the culprits? Are we ready to examine and eventually to change our consumer habits, our inclination to all kinds of waste? Have we that sound relationship with the created reality which is based on adoration of God in spirit and truth? Are we willing to take our share of responsibility to promote a radical change of public opinion and life-style?

Who does not see that these questions have much to do with the universal vocation to holiness? With our personal vocation? The world is badly in need of saints; there are so many blind guides of blind people! The world needs prophets, not only verbal protests.

The new asceticism to which we are called is not at all the punishment of our body but a new kind of fasting, renunciation, temperance as part of a life-style marked by simplicity and the joys inherent in it. And a part of today's formation of conscience is an alert and competent ecological consciousness combined with that creativity which discovers vital expressions of the new awareness.

If we seek and cultivate joy in God, the spirit of adoration and praise, the inner peace and charism of peace-makers; if we cherish the final hope based on the divine promises and on the many images we find in a healthy environment; if we are praying more for wisdom than for success, power and wealth: then we will no longer need so many things as our wasteful culture seems to need. And when parents are attentive enough to give themselves and their authentic love to their children, then they no longer need to give them the thousand useless or unnecessary things as substitutes for the missing love. Thus children, too, will develop in a healthier environment.

Whoever clearly and sincerely faces the ecological problems of today's and tomorrow's world will see most of the moral questions in a new light.

*   *   *

Lord Jesus Christ, you have come to adore the Father, in the name of all humanity and all creatures, by the full truth of life, and thus to teach us 'adoration in spirit and truth'. Open our eyes, our hearts and minds to see, with you, the beauty and destiny of creation. We intend henceforth to remember more consciously that all things are created in you, the eternal Word, and that you have taken the flesh of the earth to redeem the world. We want to thank you by our life for having taught us to nurture healthy relationships among all people and with all the reality entrusted to our stewardship.

Help us, O Lord, to strive more for wisdom, knowledge of salvation and discernment than for power and wealth. Help us to fulfil our firm purpose to use the earthly heritage in solidarity with the poor and in responsibility for future generations.

Enlighten the men and women who have special competence in problems concerning the human biosphere and ecosphere. Guide with your wisdom those who have to make grave decisions in the economic and political realm. Help them to face realistically the ecological problems and to resolve them wisely in co-operation with all people of good will.

We cannot hope for a radical change and a healthy ecological future without conversion. So we pray: Lord, forgive us our sins against your creation, against the earth and the future generations, our coveting more possessions, more consumption. And forgive us our cowardly silence while faced with all the dangerous aberrations of our culture.

H

CHAPTER EIGHTEEN

Dedication to culture

"It is like a man going abroad, who called his servants and put his capital in their hands; to one he gave five bags of gold, to another two, to another one, each according to his capacity. Then he left the country. The man who had five bags went at once and employed them in business, and made a profit of five bags, and the man who had the two bags made two. But the man who had been given one bag of gold went off and dug a hole in the ground, and hid his master's money. A long time afterwards their master returned, and proceeded to settle accounts with them. The man who had been given the five bags of gold came and produced the five he had made: 'Master,' he said, 'you left five bags with me; look, I have made five more.' 'Well done, my good and trusty servant!' said the master. 'You have proved trustworthy in a small way: I will now put you in charge of something big. Come and share your master's delight' " (Mt 25 : 14–21).

MAN'S history arises from nature and culture. Essentially, we are cultural beings, enabled and enriched by culture and devoted to culture. Surely, then, all of us should invest the talents we have received from God and make them fruitful for ourselves, our neighbours and future generations by promoting a culture that favours healthy personal relationships, the growth of creative liberty and fidelity, and an ordering of the environment that actualizes truth, goodness and beauty.

The realm of culture does not belong to only the direct cult of beauty and artistic expression of the great dimensions of human life; it includes also the shape of the landscape, the style of living, the decoration of one's home. As we have just seen, one of the greatest achievements of culture is a responsible attitude towards the milieu, the whole ordering of the environment in view of health and wholeness of persons and communities.

The programming and development of the economic structures, processes and dynamics in view of justice and peace are among man's greatest arts, although he frequently fails because of a lack of vision of wholeness which is the heart of all cultural goals. Even a good house-economy, totally ordered to the good of the family, is a manifestation of wisdom and competence. National and international economics comprise an enormous task with a decisive impact on the lives of millions of people: on their human relationships, the order or disorder of their values, and on peace.

Christians who feel a vocation in the field of culture, economics or politics, and who possess the vision of wholeness and the necessary qualities of character, as well as the necessary competence to serve the common good, justice and peace, are surely among the faithful servants to whom the Lord and Giver of talents promises a place at the feast table when the great day of accounting has arrived.

Our dedication to the promotion of culture in its various fields and dimensions should be an expression of gratitude for the talents entrusted to us by God, for the cultural inheritance from the past and for our willingness to serve the present and future generations. There is so much to be grateful for! There are the wisdom and life-experiences inherent in the many languages, including our own, the traditions, customs, wise laws and innumerable monuments of the various arts in which deep reflections and insights about the problems of life are embodied.

But all this does not help us and the future generations if we do not make individual and collective efforts to appreciate, understand, interiorize and vitalize it in view of present opportunities. The teacher of the moral law, and all who want to fulfil their role in the on-going history of salvation have to be "like a householder who can produce from his store both the new and the old" (Mt 13 : 52).

Moral and religious geniuses, prophets and saints who discover new values or fresh ways to embody traditional values according to their scale and urgency, while continuing to call for the realization of the highest personal values, are among the greatest promoters of culture when human situations, needs and possibilities are changing. Even if no art-piece of theirs will be on show in future museums, they will have helped human persons

115

themselves to become the highest result of human culture, the most precious masterpiece.

Those of us who are not experts in any specific art can be great artists nevertheless, if we truly become an image of God in love, justice, peace and the ennobling of human relationships. Living according to our faith, being open to all values, exercising discernment, remaining faithful to our conscience, and searching always for truth, goodness and truthful solutions to our problems, we make a fruitful contribution to culture without explicitly thinking in terms of culture.

In view of the great relevance of culture in all its dimensions, however, and for the well-being and dignity of all men and women, each of us, according to our own possibilities, should give explicit attention to the promotion of culture so that its decisive benefits are shared with all people, especially the poor.

In order to make a realistic contribution in a common effort we shall try to discern what, in our society and culture, serves to benefit the human person and healthy relationships, and what harms them. Our mission to be 'light to the world' and 'salt to the earth' can also request from us a critical evaluation of our culture, as well as the best possible contribution for sound public opinions, which are such an important dimension of culture.

It is an undeniable fact that in the course of history religion has made great contributions to the promotion of culture in almost all fields. The cultural fecundity of faith depends particularly on the encounter of joyous faith with genius. Orthodoxy and piety alone are not enough. The faithful Christian should also mobilize the creative capacities entrusted to him or her for the benefit of all. The believer's irreplaceable contribution is a vision of wholeness, vigilance for the signs of the times and a convincing embodiment of faith in one's daily life.

One of the basic paradigms for the Christian's involvement in culture is the incarnation of the Word of God. Jesus is born an Israelite and grew in his humanity into that culture. His horizon of thought, use of language and vision of history are indebted to the tradition of his people. The best of that culture, marked by God-experience and by prophetic actualization, comes to its fullness in him, the Son-of-man, 'one-of-us'. He did not invent all the religious and moral values which he lived and proclaimed in a totally new way. Rather, he has brought home all the treasures of the religious and moral culture of Israel into his own unique mission in the fullness of time.

Jesus does not allow any kind of monopoly by Jewish culture, not even in the religious dimension. He often praises the faith of people who do not belong to that culture. The apostle to the Gentiles explains this in view of the common calling of both Jews and Gentiles to the new covenant in Christ. Man-made barriers have to be removed so that the good in all cultures can be appreciated and brought into this wholeness. "All that is true, all that is noble, all that is just and pure, all that is lovable and gracious, whatever is excellent and admirable — fill all your thoughts with these things" (Phil 4 : 8).

Faithful to his mission, Paul can say: "To Jews I became like a Jew, to win Jews; as they are subject to the Law of Moses, I put myself under that law to win them, although I am not myself subject to it. To win Gentiles, who are outside the Law, I made myself like one of them, although I am not in truth outside God's law . . . Indeed, I have become everything in turn to men of every sort . . . All this I do for the sake of the Gospel" (1 Cor 9 : 20–22). "I am under obligation to Greek and non-Greek, to learned and simple" (Rom 1 : 14).

The Second Vatican Council insists that the church must be incarnated in the various cultures and that "the community of the faithful must be rooted in the life of the respective society and somehow adapted to the local culture" (*The Church's Missionary Activity*, 19).

An effort in this direction must also be made constantly in the countries of the old Christendom. There we meet a new culture. The spirit of evangelical poverty requires us not to cling to traditional forms where this would darken the newness of life in Christ and our mission to be salt to the earth. Christians are to be neither the last trailers entering a new culture from a great distance nor the blind followers of the new only because it is new.

If faith is deeply rooted in the hearts and minds of the faithful then, by exemplary vigilance for the signs of the times, they will 'use to the full the present opportunities' to make their encounter with the various cultures and subcultures creative and redemptive. By a ready willingness to appreciate all the good in one's own and in others' cultures, and by bringing it home into the full vision of faith and wholeness, we become better able to face the shadows of our own culture, to purify what needs to be purified and to oppose what contradicts human dignity. Thus, for example, Christians who live in a culture inclined to violence and prepotence will give particular attention to non-violence and non-violent methods to solve conflicts. In an unculture of greed and intemperate consumerism and wastefulness, they will cultivate generosity in their engagement with the poor and simplicity in their own life-style.

*   *   *

We praise you, Father, Lord of heaven and earth, for having given to humankind such wonderful capacities to cultivate the earth, to till the garden you have entrusted to us, and to care for it. You have given skill and a sense of beauty to craftsmen and have gifted many for the highest art. Song and music are your gifts and people's joy. Above all, we thank you for having called us to be coartists with you who want all men and women to become masterpieces of goodness, love, peace, wisdom and beauty.

We thank you for the rich cultural heritage of our nation and of all peoples, for the unique opportunity in our era when cultures can fertilize each other and cultivate unity in variety as well as variety in unity. Let all feel that gratitude can be best expressed by creative fidelity and responsibility in view of the present and the future generations.

Assist your church throughout the world to remain faithful to the basic experience of the first Pentecost, and to proclaim the gospel in all languages to all cultures. Free Christians everywhere, but above all in powerful nations, from any kind of cultural superiority complex. Lord, help us all to be faithful stewards in the promotion of culture.

CHAPTER NINETEEN

Present-day economics and the economy of the beatitudes

" 'So I say to you, use your worldly wealth to win friends for yourselves, so that when money is a thing of the past you may be received into an eternal home.

'The man who can be trusted in little things can be trusted also in great; and the man who is dishonest in little things is dishonest also in great things. If, then, you have not proved trustworthy with the wealth of this world, who will trust you with the wealth that is real? And if you have proved untrustworthy with what belongs to another, who will give you what is your own?

'No servant can be the slave of two masters; for either he will hate the first and love the second, or he will be devoted to the first and think nothing of the second. You cannot serve God and Money' " (Lk 16 : 9–13).

"Set your mind on God's kingdom and his justice before everything else, and all the rest will come to you as well" (Mt 6 : 33).

FOR today's Christians, even more than for the first generation of Christ's disciples, active participation in economic life is imperative. It should be a profound and clear decision, a fundamental option. Only if we set our minds thoroughly on God's kingdom and his saving justice can we gain true freedom in the economic realm and fulfil our liberating mission.

Once we have made our option for the vision of the beatitudes, we also gradually rid ourselves of our blindness, and realize painfully how frequently and how easily economic success and power are associated with 'unjust mammon', with sinful economic structures and degrading exploitation and relationships.

Christians will not bedevil the whole economic realm, as the Qumram sect did in Jesus' time, but we live a kind of exodus from all complicity with greed or the reckless striving for wealth and economic power that is detrimental to the majority of people. We do not seek, however, an exodus which would betray our mission to be 'salt to the earth' and salt also to socio-economic life.

The exodus leaves behind covetousness and idolatry of wrong economic values and brings us to creative and constructive participation. This is a prerequisite for being 'light to the world'. 'Be very sure of this: no one given to fornication or indecency, or the greed which makes an idol of gain, has any share in the kingdom of Christ and of God" (Eph 5 : 5).

I am afraid that those traditionalist Christians who 'make an idol of gain' while fighting for a severe sexual morality do not realize that they are as accountable for their particular sin as those who are 'given to fornication and indecency.' Therefore, they cannot 'have a share in the kingdom of Christ and of God.' I think that the most common aberration is still that of Christians who are given to greed in its various forms and, alas, with an all-too-good conscience.

The modern development of economics is, in one way, a monumental achievement which allows our spaceship Earth to feed more than four billion people and soon perhaps six billion. A majority of citizens of the highly industrialized nations lives in abundance. But modern economics has also failed terribly in the matter of just distribution. Hundreds of millions of people live in misery, suffering starvation as Lazarus did at the threshold of the rich reveller. The sad reason is that, since the surge of capitalism, economic life is populated by sinister idols and ideologies in both East and West.

For many people, economic activity is governed exclusively by the motives of material success, efficiency, gain and power. Classical liberalism presented the ideology which could justify this approach while also giving a good conscience to the successful. It taught that the economic realm has to develop according to its own dynamics and motives and should not be disturbed by moral imperatives. Its promise was that the egotism of the individuals and groups would guarantee the best possible success and allow the interplay of supply and demand.

Many who call themselves Christians have followed the same reasoning, at least in practice. And if some uneasiness of conscience still remained, they have tried to quiet and console it by almsgiving and pious or humanitarian philanthropies. These would pay a kind of modest tithing from the profits gathered by an unjust mammon under an unjust economic system which allows heartless exploitation of the weak.

Classical marxism adopted from this liberalism the ideology of autonomy of the economic realm adding, however, some new and particularly dangerous dimensions. In marxism, economy has not only its own iron laws of dynamics and processes but is also the determining factor for the whole of social life. It is true that marxism found private egotism at fault, not morally however, but only as a necessary result of the institution of private property. It rejects an ethical foundation of socialism, since the inborn 'law' in its ideology of socio-economic life is class war and class hatred as the dynamic of historical development. In the existing systems of marxism the machinery of state-capitalism functions even more heartlessly than capitalism with its private ownership of productive capital.

All these ideologies have espoused the evil of reckless armament which has become possible through technical and economic expansion. Its explosive risks are increased by the theory and practice of class wars, whereby the 'real marxism' in power combines ruthless oppression of the working-class with a kind of messianic class war and war against other systems.

We may not overlook, however, the fact that, side by side with the bitter fruits of 'unjust mammon', some important social gains have been made possible by the free social-market system and by some socialist states. In many countries there are insurances for times of sickness and unemployment, guarantees of place of employment and for post-retirement, and in some countries increasing participation by employees in the decision-making process and sharing in the collective gain. Considerable but still insufficient efforts are being made to humanize labour.

The Christian knows by experience about the presence of the 'sin of the world' in the economic realm, the bias of economic systems which, in theory and practice, block out the vision of redemption of economic man. Temptations have taken the form of harmful structures confirmed by no less harmful ideologies. Through the powerful channels of the mass media, strange commandments are inculcated: thou shalt covet, buy more, consume more, show off more!

Yet, believers may not doubt that redemption wrought by Jesus Christ is offered also to economic man. Therefore, they will recognize all efforts for more justice, co-humanity, peace, and temperance as signs of hope for redemption and liberation. While we have to face frankly the dangerous idols and ideologies, we ought to have open eyes and hearts for all efforts directed towards an authentic culture in the economic realm.

We do realize that unjust and unhealthy economic structures favour sinful and criminal practices; but instead of blaming all economic evils on structures, and thus practically excusing the culprits, we have to see the widespread criminality in economic life as an ethical question. Whatever structures have to be changed, we most urgently need to sharpen the consciences of all, while seeking social remedies.

Empirical studies show the shocking extent of unethical and criminal conduct in business. Many managers and owners confine their conduct to mere borderline morality, constantly lowering their standards. Meanwhile, powerful groups in industry and business block, by unfair means, legislation to set a minimum of legally-required honesty and justice.

The basic evil is that too many people are not anxious to act ethically but only to avoid conflict with penal laws. They seem to be 'honest' only insofar as this promises more for their profit-oriented business activity. But perhaps we can still think that the majority of employees, executives and managers can be counted more or less among those whom the Lord praises as faithful servants (Lk 16:9–12). Christians can be 'salt to the earth' in the economic realm only if they are absolutely honest and reliable, even when this requires sacrifices and brings disadvantages.

Yet in today's world even this does not suffice. Each and all of us, in prudent and courageous cooperation, ought to do our best to heal public life and particularly the economic culture, beginning with our own household and extending to the promotion of a new economic world order. For this purpose we shall give due attention to the social doctrines of the church and all hopeful initiatives. Here, too, there must be knowledge, competence, cooperation and the ever-necessary good will.

The enormous tasks in this field can be faced only by solidly united and competent Christians in cooperation with all people of good will. The goals are:

Application of the basic principles of social justice;

a worldwide solidarity, especially among all who participate in economic life;

subsidiarity which requires the highest possible level of sharing in decision-making processes concerning people's own well-being and that of the powerless;

justice for the ageing and retired;

effective application of equal dignity and equal rights for women in professional and industrial life;

fair and generous cooperation between the highly-industrialized, wealthy countries and the poor developing nations.

Whoever intends to content himself by honestly earning and spending his money while standing aside, as though he could exercise a beneficial influence simply by his own sense of justice, discernment and competence, has not yet understood that the calling to salvation and holiness implies essentially also mission, *action*, 'to be salt to the earth'.

Some excuse themselves by saying that nothing can be changed for the better. This pessimism is in reality a denial of the message that redemption coming from the Lord is plentiful. It denies Christ as Saviour of the world, in favour of a heretically narrow image of 'a saviour only of souls'. Of course, it is also a matter of saving one's soul, but those who do not intend to co-operate in the salvation of people in all their dimensions and relationships, who do not accept their vocation to heal public life, also ruin their own souls.

The affirmation of one's own coresponsibility in public life, including the economic realm, has much to do with the decisive criteria which the Saviour and Judge of the world indicated for the Day of Judgement (cf. Mt 25 : 31–46). Working together to heal public life, we can prevent and heal many wounds and can effectively do the works of mercy and saving justice of which the gospel speaks.

Private charity, important though it is, cannot outweigh one's grave neglect of cooperation for a better ordering of the economic life which, in its present bad shape, inflicts so many wounds, makes so many people lonely prisoners of a system, submits countless people to hunger and starvation, and deprives many of decent care, clothing and housing. . . .

By our life-style and in other ways we are involved in unjust and harmful economic structures and dynamics. Individual conversion, however, which always takes precedence, implies more than personal disentanglement. What is needed is that all those converted and on the road to conversion should work in solidarity for a profound change in our economic culture (unculture?), and ask themselves and each other some questions:

Can we liberate ourselves and others from the still-prevailing ideology of quantitative growth (growth mania) and offer instead concrete, realistic and at the same time idealistic ways to qualitative growth?

Are we willing to give concrete evidence that alternative ways of a simple life-style are possible and even attractive?

Can we give personal witness that a moderate use of material goods brings more happiness and peace than wastefulness and covetousness?

Can we help each other to read the signs of the times and to acknowledge that the present trend to ever-greater wastefulness of irreplaceable resources of energy and rare raw materials can no longer continue without grave injustice to future generations and even to our own generation?

Why could we not make the wealthy people and nations realize that they live on the same spaceship as the poorest people and nations who are claiming loudly their rightful share as compared with our inordinate consumption?

Should we not combine the art of dialogue and competence in influencing public opinions in this field with a convincing life-style?

If we lack the courage and creative initiatives to take these steps, we have to wonder whether our faith in redemption, our faith in the Redeemer of the world, is alive enough.

After all, we do not forget that, at best, we are underway in our conversion and setting out for solidly-united actions of renewal. What is urgently needed is the clear goal and common effort to find, day by day, the next step in the right direction towards a socio-economic order of sobriety, an economy that serves real needs instead of creating artificial and harmful needs, a better distribution of time of work and leisure in view of over-coming unemployment, and an economic style which allows creativity and joy in the common work.

The sermon on the mount does not give us a concrete model of modern economy; it offers no panacea for resolving the increasing north-south conflict. But it shows us a clear direction for the attitudes which believers need in order to be 'light to the world', attitudes which will be also the best foundation for a sincere search for the ways and the next possible steps to be taken.

We can somehow sum up what would be brought about by a radical conversion to an 'economy of the beatitudes':

Where people believe in the kingdom of God and set their minds on God's saving justice before all else, there the weak and poor no longer are degraded and exploited.

Where disciples of Christ hunger and thirst for God's justice, there the greed for more money and more power over others fades away.

Where believers practise Christ's gentleness, there the key is found for the solution of conflicts.

Where people faithfully and gratefully praise the God of mercy, there is no room for the idol of class-hatred as bearer of 'progress'; there is no place for collective selfishness; the handi-capped are no longer marginal people.

Where believers' hearts are purified by the experience of God's love, there will grow a sympathetic understanding of people's true needs.

Where men and women see their highest bliss and honour in being children of God, there will be a total commitment to peace, justice and reconciliation.

Where people truly believe the message of the gospel, there will be brave souls like Bishop Romero of El Salvador and thousands of others who are ready to suffer persecution and death for the sake of authentic peace and saving justice. And despite temporary lack of success, they will not lose hope for they have entrusted themselves to God.

All this is an essential part of the christian calling and mission: "You are salt to the earth" (Mt 5:15).

The message of the sermon on the mount to 'put away

anxious thoughts about food and drink' and the invitation to look at the 'birds of the air and the lilies of the fields' are in no way a call to withdraw into private quietude and interests. Rather, they call us to the all-encompassing vocation to set our minds on God's kingdom before anything else (cf. Mt 6 : 25–33).

Wonderful things could happen in the realm of economics, culture and politics if we Christians would believe the gospel with all our hearts and, as people renewed by this spirit, would set out for ways to make the gospel a reality. A great expert in economics, E. F. Schumacher, is convinced that this is what the world needs above all else.

*   *   *

Lord Jesus Christ, you call yourself the 'bread for the life of the world'. You live and die for others and teach us to ask the Father for our daily bread, the bread for all, which unites people. Convert us by the power of your Spirit so that, together and in mutual service, we may set out to work and to order our socio-economic relationships in a way that honours the treasures of the earth and the fruit of our labour, as gifts from the one Father of all.

Lord, free people in the realm of labour and business from greed and alienation. Help us to discover your design for salvation also in the realm of economics. Grant us wisdom and courage to work for the healing of economic man and economic structures from the wounds of greed and lust for power. Give the world saints who show us what it really means to believe in you as the Saviour of the world.

Our Father, Father of all, let the world see people who have set their minds first to honour your name, to wait and to work, to pray and to suffer for the coming of your kingdom, people who seek in all things your will, who pray and work for the bread of all your children, who learn from you generous and healing forgiveness and unite themselves in efforts to remove the terrible temptations from the economic reality: people who, above all, believe in plentiful redemption and therefore commit themselves to the liberation of all men and women from the terrible evil that besets our world.

CHAPTER TWENTY

Christians and politics

"Jesus answered (the devil), 'Scripture says again, "You are not to put the Lord your God to the test." '

Once again, the devil took him to a very high mountain, and showed him all the kingdoms of the world in their glory. 'All these,' he said, 'I will give you, if you will only fall down and do me homage.' But Jesus said, 'Begone, Satan! Scripture says, "You shall do homage to the Lord your God and worship him alone." '

Then the devil left him; and angels appeared and waited on him" (Mt 4:7–11).

"Every person must submit to the supreme authorities. There is no authority but by act of God, and the existing authorities are instituted by him; consequently anyone who rebels against authority is resisting a divine institution, and those who so resist have themselves to thank for the punishment they will receive. For government, a terror to crime, has no terrors for good behaviour. You wish to have no fear of the authorities? Then continue to do right and you will have their approval, for they are God's agents working for your good. But if you are doing wrong, then you will have cause to fear them; it is not for nothing that they hold the power of the sword, for they are God's agents of punishment, for retribution on the offender. That is why you are obliged to submit. It is an obligation imposed not merely by fear of retribution but by conscience. That is also why you pay taxes. The authorities are in God's service and to these duties they devote their energies.

"Discharge your obligations to all men; pay tax and toll, reverence and respect, to those to whom they are due" (Rom. 13:1–7).

TO have an idea of how much can be accomplished by good and capable politicians, think of such men as Robert Schuman, Alcide de Gasperi, Konrad Adenauer who, marked by christian faith and great competence, worked with all their conviction and skill for the reconciliation of their nations and for European solidarity. Then think of the stupidity of those who voted for Hitler in 1933 or entered into alliances with his party because of collective and personal egotism, and of those who brought Stalin to power and sustained him in it. Think of the millions of citizens who simply neglected their political responsibility and thus let evil prevail and continue.

In the earliest christian era, when the small minority of Christians could not even dream of exercising a positive influence in the political arena, simple people could do little more than quietly fulfil their civil duties and offer prayers "for sovereigns and all in high office, that we may lead a tranquil and quiet life in full observance of religion and high standards of morality" (1 Tim 2:2). For the rest, Christians had to be instructed on the meaning and limits of dutiful obedience to political rulers and civil laws.

The texts of the Bible offer a somewhat clear direction only in their totality. On the one hand, they affirm responsible obedience; on the other, they unmask and condemn abuse of political power.

The insistence on obedience is found especially in Paul's letter to the Romans and in the first letter of Peter. In the latter it is evident that a chief motive for the text is to show that Christians were unjustly accused of being enemies of the Roman Empire, enemies of the state. "Submit yourselves to every human institution for the sake of the Lord, whether to the sovereign as supreme, or the governor as his deputy for the punishment of criminals and the commendation of those who do right. For it is the will of God that by your good conduct you should put ignorance and stupidity to silence" (1 Pet 2:13–15).

There are also good reasons to see in the text of the epistle to the Romans, quoted above, an apologetic intention and a reassurance to the political powers that they have nothing to fear from Christians. But in both cases the evident concern is that Christians give support to the common good by exemplary fulfilment of their duties to the political authorities and just laws. Paul's insistence that it is "an obligation imposed not merely by fear of retribution but by conscience" (Rom 13:5) indicates the kind of obligation but also its limits. Nobody is allowed to offer the state an obedience that is against an upright conscience.

The church's position on political power in biblical times was primarily critical. Jesus himself, *the* Prophet, continues and fulfils the prophetic tradition which unmasked and chastised the abuse of power and any kind of exploitation and oppression of the weak and poor. If Jesus had spoken only of the salvation of souls, the leaders of Israel and the Roman deputy would have left him in peace. He gave a frank characterization of Herod when he called him a 'fox' (cf. Lk 13 : 32).

Jesus shows prophetic wrath at the sight of terrible abuse of religious authority by the leaders of the Jews. He saw himself surrounded by satanic temptation arising from a mixture of religion and lust for power. This temptation approaches him in a penetrant way through those who are misled by an earthly messianic expectation. The story of the temptations makes evident how shameless Jesus considered this kind of temptation and how sharply he opposed it (cf. Mt 4 : 7–11).

His attitude becomes even clearer in his harsh correction of Peter when this privileged apostle, who had just acknowledged Jesus as the Messiah, proved to be misled by an erroneous expectation of a Messiah who would submit people by sheer power. Contaminated by this widespread error, Peter could not yet accept a meek, powerless, suffering 'servant-of-God'. In this context Jesus calls Peter even 'Satan' and a 'stumbling block' (cf. Mt 16 : 21–23).

As witnesses to the nearness of the kingdom of God, the disciples of Jesus are urged to develop attitudes directly opposed to those of kings and powerful men of this world (cf. Lk 22 : 24–27). If all Christians were to observe these directives, then the great prophecies of the coming of God's kingdom would become more evident. Then the ancient fights among believers for power, privileges and arrogant titles would be finally ended, unmasked in their nonsense, to the benefit also of the political realm.

The history of humanity right up to our own times is filled with wrong and dangerous messianic expectations, and not only in the new Israelitic state whose fate may yet depend upon this point. Sadly we remember the appalling theory of Boniface VIII and others regarding the 'two swords of the church', the acceptance by Innocent III of the title of Latin emperor of Constantinople given to him by the crusaders, all the 'holy' wars, the wars of the Spanish crown against the Indians who were not ready to

I

accept baptism as a sign of submission to enforced labour, the wars of usurpation waged by the protestant colonizers against the North American aborigines. All were based on a wrong concept of chosenness over and against others.

History tells us of numerous forms of secularized offspring of these ideas of 'chosen nations' in the political and economic wars in Europe. We think also of the principle of USA politicians who insisted on 'unconditional surrender' of the Germans and Japanese, leading finally to the 'moral justification' of the use of atom bombs against open cities in Japan. There are also the apartheid politics in South Africa and, last but not least, Hitler's holocaust for his myth of a 'chosen' race.

With good reason historians see, in the outrageous aberrations of the Kremlin's marxism, a strange mixture of the messianic ideas of the Russia of the Czars and the pan-slavism on the one hand and, on the other, the secularized messianism of Karl Marx, who announced a golden era as a result of class struggle in the dialectic evolution.

Imperialism, militarism and intolerance in their worst forms have been the bitter fruits of some kinds of false religion and/or secularized ideologies of redemption. All this falls under the perspectives of Jesus' tearful cry: "If only you had known, on this great day, the way that leads to peace!" (Lk 19:42).

True disciples of Christ know that they can think and speak of 'chosenness', in their calling to holiness and their mission to be 'light to the world', only in humble discipleship of the Prince of Peace, the Servant of God and humankind, Jesus Christ. Nothing is more needed for the redemption of the political realm than Christians who bring home this vision of faith by witness and responsible activity.

The frequently quoted and misunderstood words of Jesus, "Then pay Caesar what is due to Caesar, and pay to God what is due to God" (Mt 22:21; Mk 12:17; Lk 20:25), should be understood in the context as a sharp rejection of the cult of the emperor by the first generations of Christians, although at the same time they also affirmed 'due submission'. Whoever pays to God what is due to God, adoring him alone and adoring him in all one's life (cf. Mt 4:10), will make his contribution to the common good but will never yield to the cult of sovereigns and states.

The texts of the New Testament regarding political ethics have to be read within this tension. Christians are by no means anarchists, but if they follow the great prophetic tradition culminating in Christ, they will never be submissive followers of dictators, imperialists or militarists.

We cannot overlook the song of praise of the humble handmaid, the mother of Jesus, who is thoroughly marked by this prophetic vision: "The arrogant of heart and mind he has put to rout, he has brought down monarchs from their thrones" (Lk 1:52). The Book of Revelation, with its arrant rejection of any form of cult of earthly power or of emperors, gives us the picture of the church insofar as she follows Mary and the Servant-Messiah. She is a great sign of salvation in contrast to the dragon with his "seven heads and seven diadems on them . . . flung to the earth" (Rev 12:1-4).

The great question is: will Christians of today and tomorrow embody the prophetic tension between creative loyalty and prophetic frankness in the realm of politics? If Christians realize how important competent engagement is in the political arena and also believe firmly in their vocation to holiness, then we can hope that the world will be blessed by men and women who are both saints and competent actors in the realm of politics.

Revelation instructs us about the sharp tension between the original design of the Creator, the fallenness of humankind and the fact of redemption. The decisive word is *redemption*. Believers, whose whole life praises the gift of redemption, will discover gradually the design of the Creator and Redeemer and will be able to face the reality of 'the sin of the world'.

Power — and especially absolute power — is exposed to the sharpest temptations. History shows us that this is true of both political and religious powers. The organization of the church and the exercise of religious authority in the church are not to be made in the image of political powers.

The Second Vatican Council emphasizes the otherness of the successors of the apostles. They proclaim the gospel "in the power of God, who very often reveals the might of the gospel through the weakness of its witnesses. For, those who dedicate themselves to the ministry of God's Word should use means and helps proper to the gospel. In many respects these differ from the supports of the earthly city" (*The Church in the Modern World*, 76).

By fidelity to the gospel Christians, who are at the same time citizens of the earthly city and of the kingdom of God, can exercise great influence in unmasking the temptations of power and showing the ways of saving-solidarity. The Christian does not bedevil the political power as such, but he will be vigilant and cal for vigilance against the pitfalls and temptations to which it is constantly exposed.

The battle against our individual and collective egotism and against all kinds of lust for power goes hand in hand with a creative effort for political renewal. Our fight against our personal sinfulness is inseparable from the fight against the 'sin of the world', especially insofar as it is manifested in abuse of power and authority. We cannot overlook the fact that, on the one hand, the field of politics is a hotbed of the 'sin of the world' and, on the other hand, Christians should see how much good their redemptive presence could do in this arena.

An intelligent and faithful application of the principle of subsidiarity on all levels is one of the most effective antidotes for the temptations of power. This fundamental principle of catholic social ethics implies a widespread and organic distribution of power, whereby it is always subordinate to participation, service and coresponsibility.

There must be room for individual initiatives. What the family can fulfil meaningfully must not be usurped by the political community. The purpose of family politics is, above all, to strengthen the family's own functions. What the lower level can do should not be taken over by the higher level of political, social or economic organization. If urgent needs of the common good or evident inabilities require the higher levels to assume functions which would be ordinarily performed at a lower level, then every effort must be made to restore conditions which allow the lower to perform the functions. All trends towards centralism must be considered abnormal as soon as they are opposed to subsidiarity.

If the principle of subsidiarity functions well on all levels, strengthening personal responsibility and protecting against temptations to disproportionate power, then we can favour and foster a development towards a world-authority without the otherwise justified fear that this might degenerate into 'the animal from the abyss', an all-devouring moloch of power.

For these and other reasons, the social doctrine of recent popes has favoured a development towards democracy, insofar as this is historically possible. We can speak of an authentic democracy when there is a widespread distribution of power, observance of the principle of subsidiarity in a federative organization, and when a party and government are elected for only a specific time. Free elections at regular intervals must allow the population to give approval or disapproval, to give opportunities to other parties and coalitions, and to indicate the main principles of the desired programmes.

Democracy is built on the principle of tolerance and free participation of all in the formation of public opinion. Of course, political tolerance has its limits wherever a group or party intends to take absolute power and to deprive the majority of the population of its participation.

The proper functioning of democracy is unthinkable without a thorough political formation of the whole population. No party, no government must be allowed a monopoly in political formation, for this would imply manipulation in favour of a group pretending to permanent or absolute power.

Political formation includes formation of a political conscience. Citizens must know the values at stake in political decisions and by what scale of values they should evaluate the decisions. A politically mature conscience knows the proper goals of political activity, the needs of the common good and the need to seek, in shared responsibility, the best possible means to reach the right goals. In a sinful world it implies also a sharp awareness of the dangers of individual and collective egotisms. There must be a constant effort towards better and better political realization and a readiness for self-criticism by the individuals and groups involved. Yet, in striving towards an ideal order, we must not forget that politics in an imperfect and sinful world requires always the 'art of the possible'.

By casting our vote, by speaking out our position on political programmes, and by participating in the formation of public opinions, there must be a constant awareness of the common good. While never losing sight of the ideal goals, a sense of realism helps us to choose the best possible solution which sometimes means the least imperfect one. As long as we continue to work in the right direction, the 'art of the possible' is no betrayal of conscience.

*   *   *

God, Father of all, open our consciences for political responsibility, for political formation as the duty of all of us. Grant us the gifts of wisdom and discernment.

Free us from narrowness, from the chains of collective egotism as well as from individualism. Grant us, along with love for our country, a sense of worldwide solidarity and readiness for planetary cooperation.

Give us men and women with a genuine political vocation, able to fulfil a political role in our communities, in our country and in international organizations with competence and wisdom.

CHAPTER TWENTY-ONE

Called for peace

"Come, let us climb up on to the mountain of the Lord,
to the house of the God of Jacob,
that he may teach us his ways
and we may walk in his paths.
For instruction issues from Zion
and out of Jerusalem comes the word of the Lord;
he will be judge between nations,
arbiter among many peoples.
They shall beat their swords into mattocks
and their spears into pruning-knives;
nation shall not lift sword against nation
nor ever again be trained for war" (Is 2:3–4).

"Salt is a good thing; but if the salt loses its saltness, what will you season it with?
Have salt in yourselves; and be at peace with one another" (Mk 9:50).

TO 'have salt in' ourselves means to be filled with the peace of the Lord, ready to be messengers of peace, to radiate peace. If individual Christians or a christian community lacks peace, then their being Christians is without flavour. The peace for which Christ has come and which he has promised to his disciples is a blissful gift to everyone who truly believes in him and trusts in him. And whoever receives this gift gratefully will realize that it is a gift destined for all: that one cannot be a bearer of peace without being also its messenger.

The peace of Christ is indivisible, an all-encompassing gift. It is first experienced as peace with God, "peace keeping guard over our hearts and thoughts, arbiter in our hearts" (Phil 4:7; Col 3:15). Since the Prince of Peace is the Liberator of the world from injustice, hatred and war, no one can exult in Christ's

135

peace of heart without committing oneself to the mission of peace for all people.

Peace is central in the prophetic expectation of Israel, and even more so in the New Testament which frequently is called simply 'the Gospel of Peace'. The 'Shalom' of the risen Christ lifts his disciples from sadness and fills their hearts with joy and trust. A second time he greets them, 'Shalom', giving them their mission of peace: "As the Father has sent me, so I send you" (Jn 20:21). He breathes his peace into their hearts and grants them his Spirit whose fruits are "love, joy, peace" (Gal 5:22).

An essential part of the peace mission is the proclamation of forgiveness to all who forgive (cf. Jn 20:21). The apostles of peace and reconciliation come as Christ's ambassadors (cf. 2 Cor 5:20), pleading that people should heed the hour of favour. And everyone should know that God himself will call the peacemakers his sons and daughters (cf. Mt 5:9).

The mission for peace is more than an imperative from outside. The innermost experience of the gift of peace makes the disciples of Christ yearn for all people to experience it. They pray and dedicate themselves to the work of peace.

The Bible shows that Christ is much concerned that his disciples should be able to distinguish the true peace, which he grants, from all false talk about peace. The one who brings peace does disturb people, shaking their consciences, making them aware that they are in need of genuine reconciliation and genuine peace. This shaking-up from false and even odious peace is strongly symbolized in Jesus' action in driving out from the temple those who would make religion a business.

Whoever desires the peace of Christ must break with any spirit of deception, greed or lust for power. Christ himself knows that his message will bring him an 'ordeal' (cf. Lk 12:51). His person and his message force people to make decisions which will be violently opposed by those who reject his peace (cf. Lk 12:15–53). The messengers of Christ's gospel of peace will experience what the prophet Simeon foretold at Christ's coming into the world: "The secret thoughts of many will be laid bare" (Lk 2:35).

When we hear Jesus saying to his disciples, "Peace is my parting gift to you, my own peace, such as the world cannot give" (Jn 14:27), we might think about the frequently-used word at that time, the 'Pax Romana', Roman peace, which was offered to those conquered by the sword and willing to accept colonial status.

The peace of Christ does not allow any dream of submitting people to it by the sword. The Prince of the messianic peace, exalted on the cross, wants to draw people to himself and to the Father's kingdom by the power of his non-violent love. This divine design of peace and salvation is in some way a two-edged sword. It forces our hearts to take sides for or against this peace.

There was evidently a misunderstanding of some of Christ's words and actions. Jesus, Lamb of God, going meekly on the way of suffering, was pained by the loud talk of some of his disciples about having swords for the fight. Matthew reports his words as, "I have not come to bring peace but a sword" (10:34). Luke is more precise: "I have come to bring division" (Lk 12:51). Faced with Christ, who is Peace in person, the hidden conflicts between light and darkness come out into the open.

Those who still think that swords — or now even nuclear weapons — are the proper means for the reign of light, should remember Jesus' abrupt response, "Enough, enough" (Lk 22:38) to his disciples' talk about swords. Enough of this! No more of this! It is shocking to see how often people, who call themselves Christians, continue to talk quite readily about the 'two swords', confusing the sword of the word of God with the weaponry of unredeemed man.

While Christians must unfailingly give witness to justice and peace, they must also be ready and eager to resolve conflicts by non-violent means. This is an irrenounceable part of their mission.

What is needed is a profound knowledge of Christ, the Prince of Peace, and a deep experience of the peace which he grants, in order to harmonize a prophetic frankness with the patient and difficult art of non-violent action in the struggle against deceit, exploitation and injustice. Are we willing to follow Christ in his courageous unmasking of hypocrisy and injustice? Then we must learn from him to suffer, to forgive patiently, to appeal to conscience whenever our engagements for justice, truth and peace bring us hard opposition.

Mahatma Gandhi and Martin Luther King ventured their lives and finally sacrificed them for *satyagraha*, the non-violent power of truth, love, justice and solidarity with the downtrodden. Gandhi, while not formally a Christian but a fervent disciple of Christ, was convinced that this is a central message of the sermon on the mount and the life and death of Christ.

In his *ashrams* (houses of prayer) Gandhi and his followers have implored satyagraha and trained themselves for it. It means nothing less than total dedication to the liberating truth that God is love and is the God of peace. It is faithful trust that this liberating truth, witnessed with all one's life, is more powerful than all the arrows of evil.

Part and parcel of satyagraha is the art of discovering the inmost energies of truth and love in oneself and others (including opponents), of considering them as precious gifts of God and mobilizing them by faith active in love.

This requires the courage to rid oneself of the age-old models of hatred, trust in threatening armaments, reduction of others to 'scheming enemies' who deserve nothing else than bedevilment. It means the inner strength and vital communication to let opponents, even the most threatening ones, know the truth: "In you, too, there are energies that can be awakened for truth, justice, love and peace."

At this juncture of history when we have to decide between reconciliation and annihilation of humankind, each family, each monastery, each parish, indeed, the whole church should become an *ashram,* house of prayer, where we allow the Divine Master to teach us, from within, the liberating truth of the power of the gospel of peace; houses of prayer where we learn, day by day and in the midst of struggle, the art of healthy and healing relationship, of peaceful solution of conflicts, while constantly imploring all this as a gift coming from above and taking root in all peoples' hearts.

Satyagraha, in the above sense, should be the heart of modern peace research and peace education throughout the world. Creative liberation from violent thinking, talking and action must be joined with liberation from greed, arrogance, lust for power, manipulation of persons, and from all tendencies to make people tools of our selfish purposes.

It is my firm conviction that, for Christians, only the universal, profound and purposeful exercise of the attitude and skill of satyagraha, as a concrete sign of their faith in the gospel of peace, can break the vicious circle of the armaments race. I should like to call it the most effective 'defence contract'. It is like the 'weaponry' of which the epistle to the Ephesians (chapter 6) speaks, for the fight "against cosmic powers, against the authorities and potentates of this dark world". It is part of 'God's armour'; the 'belt of truth', integrity 'for coat of mail', the gospel of peace as 'shoes on your feet . . . to give you firm footing'. We need a historical application of the "great shield of faith . . . the sword which the Spirit gives you" (Eph 6: 10–17).

Governments, systems and nations that are still imprisoned in the age-old mania to impose their will and collective egotism on other systems and nations by brutal threats of nuclear and chemical weaponry, should be brought to their senses and convinced of their wrong by communities and nations who have taken up the non-violent weaponry of satyagraha.

We need nations that are healed from the mental disease and claims of superpowers, ideologies and hatred, nations willing to withstand evil, solidly united in the spirit and art of satyagraha. Would not the armies used by oppressors and violent potentates be humbled and brought to reflection were they to see the spiritual and moral power of nations and social groups who could challenge them to learn this 'higher' art, the only real art in the fight for the reign of truth, justice and abiding peace?

Coherent satyagraha is perhaps the indispensable way to witness faith in Christ, the Prince of Peace, today. Christians should open themselves consciously to this gift of Christ. They should be leaders, while also gratefully accepting the witness of prophets like Gandhi.

All people who have the inner strength to choose satyagraha and the sacrifices implied, all who cooperate untiringly with Christians and non-Christians and prepare themselves for the faithful practice of satyagraha, are sons and daughters of God. They have already made their option for the gospel of the peace of Christ even before they might be fully conscious of this supreme choice for the kingdom of God.

Willing to fulfil the mission received from Christ, 'You are light for the world', in view of a humanity threatened by self-annihilation, Christians are to give witness to the gospel of peace by their life-style, by their relations with fellowmen, their attitude towards animals, their ecological temperance and wisdom, their commitment to a qualitative (instead of a mere quantitative) growth of the economic life, and by their peace-politics.

In each aspect and phase of life we must help each other in our own education for peace and non-violence, discovering together ever anew the beauty and resources of the gospel of peace. There are a thousand ways to give creative testimony to confirm and to spread our belief that peace is possible if we have true faith in the Prince of Peace, and to do whatever is in our power to strengthen this faith that peace is possible although not without liberating sacrifices.

A passive pacifism, which intends simply to dwell outside the conflicts of politics and other realities, is cheap. The blessed peacemakers (cf. Mt 5:9) must be present in the midst of real life, at the heart of conflict, in order to work for non-violent reconciliation. The servant of peace is ready to pay in person, without bitterness and without wavering in his faith in the gospel of peace.

Peace apostles will observe the political development in full awareness of its complexity and respond with the best possible competence, ready to cooperate with all groups and individuals who believe in the possibility of peace. They will never tire in their efforts to transform all of politics into politics of peace. This means nothing less than that, in all problems and everywhere, the concern for peace and justice takes precedence.

Anyone who wholeheartedly believes in the God of peace knows infallibly that no one may exploit or degrade another person and no group may exploit or degrade another group. If one does not know this and does not translate this belief into life, then he should be shocked about his lack of faith.

While true faith in the one God and Father of all human-kind is infallible in regard to the goal of the gospel of peace, we all are less than infallible in regard to the next step to be taken in the actual endeavour to solve and to prevent conflicts on the road to final peace. But, at least, we shall not deceive anyone about our conviction that this modest step calls for ever further steps for more justice and a more solidly grounded peace.

*   *   *

God of peace, we praise you for not abandoning a rebellious and peaceless humankind in its estrangement and self-destructiveness, but sent us your only begotten Son as Reconciler and Peace. He has shown us the ways of peace and sealed his gospel of peace by his precious blood.

Send forth your Spirit, and open our eyes and the eyes of all people to the abyss into which humankind is threatened to fall. Bring forth in us the fruits of the Spirit: truth, love, peace and justice. Let your Spirit guide us on the paths of peace.

Holy Spirit, help us to discover our inner resources for peace, which are your gifts to us, and to mobilize these energies so that we may be credible witnesses for the gospel of peace and the power of non-violent action. Give us the skill to convince all of humanity that conversion to peace is most urgent in view of the threatening power-blocks and dangerous ideologies which still dare to glorify violence, hatred and claims of superiority in weapons of cruelty and destruction.

Lord, prepare us with the weapons of love and peace, with invincible faith in the final victory of truth and love. Grant us the courage to commit ourselves to the gospel of peace, whatever may be the necessary sacrifices. Let the gospel of peace be 'the shoes on our feet' to give us firm footing. Let us experience the power of your Spirit through the power of faith to quench all the flaming arrows of evil.